A GAME OF NINES

IN

THE BATTLE OF RESACA

GEORGIA

MAY 13-15, 1864

A GAME OF NINES

IN

THE BATTLE OF RESACA

GEORGIA

MAY 13-15, 1864

BY

ROBERT G. MILLER

First Battle of Benjamin Harrison's Brigade

Distilled from
They All Wore a Star, 2e
by the Same Author

Mauvaisterre Publishing

Cover: View from the Union Position from Hazen's position. Painted immediately after the Battle of Resaca on May 15, 1864 by James Walker, Oil on Canvas, 14 ½ x 36 ½ inches. Located at the Oneida County Historical Society, 1608 Genesee Street, Utica, New York 13502. Originally hung at the U.S. War Department. Art Inventories Catalog, Smithsonian American Art Museums, Control Number IAP 38330003. This image is courtesy of Oneida County Historical Society. Digital color restoration of the painting was by Robert G. Miller. Pictured seated in center, General Howard, Commanding 4th Corps. On the right, pointing, General Hooker, Commanding 20th Corps, with General Sickles and Col. J. A. Reynolds, Chief of Artillery, according to a lithograph featuring the painting. The Red, White, and Blue Stars are of the 1st, 2nd, and 3rd Divisions of the 20th Corps of the Union Army.

The font is Warnock Pro, a classical style seen in the regimental histories and memoirs of those who fought this battle.

CONTENTS

DEDICATED

To those who fought this battle

and

those who left witness.

There was one place, though, where Sherman, had he been the able general many supposed, would have taken some of Johnston's glory from him. The only time he ever got Johnston apparently in a nine hole was at Resaca, on May 15, 1864. — Ridley, Confederate Captain

The Deadly Game of Nines

In the game of nines, each side has three pegs and tries to place them in a straight line among the nine holes of a three-sided square. It's an ancient game, like tic-tac-toe, but allows players to take turns after all pegs are on the board. On each turn a player can move one peg to a vacant hole, seeking advantage. But that leaves another hole open. When there is no choice but to leave a hole in a line where the opponent already has two pegs, the winner has the loser in a nine-hole. In the American Civil War, the opening phase of the Atlanta Campaign was played like such a game.

But this was war: fighting for position, playing out of turn, and hiding your move if you can, making deception a most powerful weapon by which an illusionist might turn weakness to advantage. So one has to adapt to the adversary's every move.

On a large battlefield, units are spread out, and communication is difficult and chancy. Commanders have to make decisions on the spot. Thus, they all need to know the plan and have the same objectives. Wrong moves can cause chaos. Chaos kills.

·Map of the·
ATLANTA
CAMPAIGN
SCALE OF MILES
MATTHEWS, NORTHRUP & CO.
·ART·PRINTING·WORKS·
BUFFALO, N.Y.

May of 1864

With the beginning of May, the grand Atlanta Campaign commenced. It is said that some of the rebels afterwards declared, Old Sherman ascended to the top of Lookout Mountain, gave the command, 'Attention! Creation! by kingdom right wheel march!' and The Yankees came down like the wolf on the fold! – Sergeant Major Fleharty

One who participated in the Atlanta Campaign explains it thus:

Captain Stephen D. Pierson, Company D, 33rd NJ: *The Spring of '64 opened very hopefully for the Union cause. In the West our successes had been most fruitful. Vicksburg had been taken—the Mississippi River was open to its mouth—everything west of it was practically lost to the Confederacy. The Rebel lines had been securely pushed back through Kentucky and Tennessee to the Georgia line, and we held Chattanooga firmly. East Tennessee and Knoxville, too, were ours.*

Grant, as Commander-in-Chief, was taking personal charge of the movements in the East, while to grand old Sherman, Uncle Billy, as we, his boys, loved to call him, was entrusted the work in the West. On both sides it was felt that the situation was an earnest one. Grant planned for a general and simultaneous advance of all the armies on May 1st. He wrote to Sherman:

Your objective is Johnston's army—mine is Lee's army. You keep Johnston so busy that he can send no help to Lee, and I will try to keep Lee so fully occupied that he can send no help to Johnston.

To oppose Johnston Sherman had 100,000 men, seemingly large odds, but the one fought behind works, carefully prepared in advance in many cases, and, as he fell back, he was, going towards his supplies and reinforcements, while we were getting farther and farther away with each victorious advance. Sherman's plan was carefully thought out in advance; in brief it was to hold Thomas with his Army of the Cumberland, 60,000 strong, in the centre, McPherson, with his Army of the Tennessee, 25,000 strong, and

Schofield, with his Army of the Ohio, 15,000 strong, on either wing, to push the enemy with strong lines wherever found, to hold him there, while with one wing or the other he pressed around one flank or the other and compelled him to retreat or to fight in the open. He reasoned that he could not afford, considering his distance from supplies and reinforcements, to waste his strength by hurling his army against entrenchments, where one man in defence is equal to at least three attacking. Victory, even if won, would be at too great a cost and leave him crippled for further offensive action.

To flank means this: When soldiers are formed in line of battle, whether in the open or behind breast works, the whole line can return the fire of the attacking party. Moreover, bullets and shot missing the line go harmlessly to the rear. But, if the attacking force goes around one end or the other of the line, only very few can get in position to return the fire, while the bullets and shot go raking down the whole line. The only thing then left to do is to change front, as it is called, by maneuvers not easy to make under fire, or else to retreat.

And so, on May 1st, Sherman's forces started for Dalton, Georgia, where Johnston's army had been holed up for the winter behind a high rocky ridge.

Sergeant Grunert, Co D 129th Ill Ward's 1st Brigade, 3rd Division, 20th Corps: *May 5. We remained in camp and in consequence of this lying idle, the fighting spirit of the men gave way to still and silent thoughts about the impenetrable future, or about the strength of the enemy in our front, estimated at 80,000 men. Letters were written to our friends and relatives at home to let them know that we were well. Although all knew that many a one would have to lose his life, or be wounded on the battlefield, or perhaps be crippled for life, yet a stern resolution was fixed in all hearts of those brave men to fight and perhaps die for the country. Such a spirit can only arise from a pure and holy love of the cause of our glorious Union! Our officers were equally brave and to be trusted, and we were certain of the final victory. We drew rations to-day for three days, and the regiment had dress parade. Several of our scouts were taken prisoner to-day.*

His brigade had witnessed the destroyed and dead after the Battles of Perryville and Stones River, and they had read of victories and defeats at Vicksburg, Gettysburg and other fights, while they endured extremes of weather on long nights of picket, hard marches, and idleness as disease took comrades. All the while, they wanted to fight, to get the war on and ended and be home.

Sherman's plan was to hold Johnston at Dalton while McPherson's Army of the Tennessee went south to block Johnston's access to his lifeline, the railroad to Atlanta. We pick up our story in Resaca several days later.

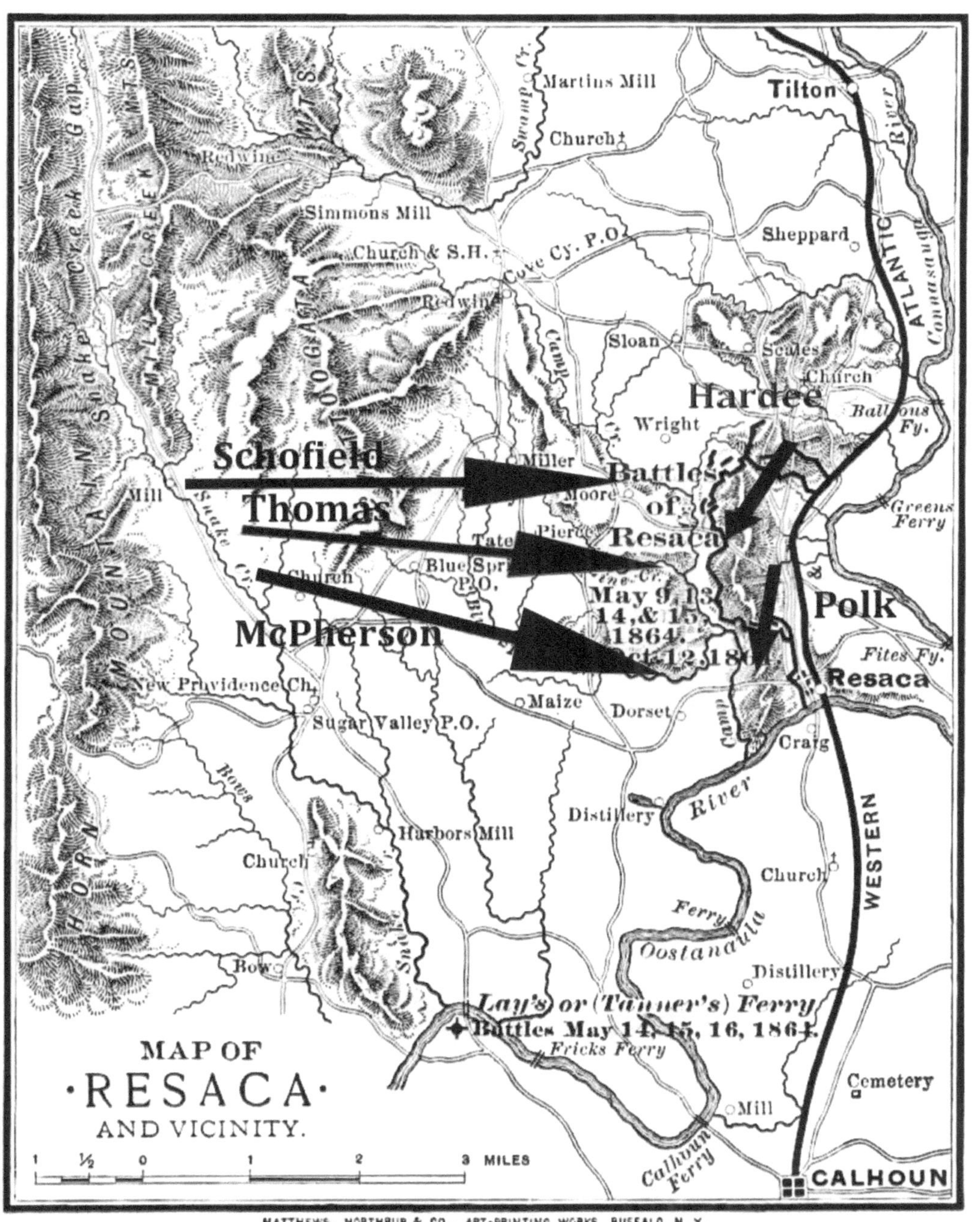

Tilton
Martins Mill
Church
Swamp Cr.
Sheppard
ATLANTIC
Comasauga River
Simmons Mill
Church & S.H.
Cove Cy. P.O.
Redwine
Redwine
Sloan
Scales
Church
Ballous Fy.
Schofield
Thomas
Miller
Moore
Pierce
Tate
Wright
Hardee
Greens Ferry
Battles of Resaca
May 9, 13, 14, & 15, 1864.
Oct. 12, 186
Polk
Mill
Snake Cr.
Church
Blue Spr. P.O.
Pine Cr.
McPherson
New Providence Ch.
Sugar Valley P.O.
Maize
Dorset
Fites Fy.
Resaca
Craig
Bows
Harbors Mill
Church
Distillery
River
Church
WESTERN
Oostanaula
Ferry
Distillery
Row
Lay's or (Tanner's) Ferry
Battles May 14, 15, 16, 1864.
Fricks Ferry
Cemetery
Mill
Calhoun Ferry
CALHOUN
MAP OF
·RESACA·
AND VICINITY.
1   ½   0   1   2   3 MILES

About Army Units

His name and his regiment were a volunteer soldier's identity. He joined a local company of about 100; and when it was mustered in as part of a regiment of ten companies his regimental home was set. Volunteer regiments were organized by a state, and officers were chosen from within. That regiment stayed intact, regardless of the larger units it might become part of.

The regiment was his war family. These comrades, being from the same area, were committed to, and depended on, each other. Pride of doing well was manifested in the regiment as a whole and in its commanders.

However, as men were lost, recruitment of new members lagged. Sometimes a member was sent home to try to find new members, but that was not sufficient. So over the term of enlistment, due to disease and battle, a regiment could be greatly reduced. After two years of battle, 500 was a large number. The 3rd Tennessee Confederate regiment and another, combined, had only 18 survivors at the end of the war.

A line of infantrymen, elbow-to-elbow, under one commander, was called a battalion. It was usually a regiment, but often more than one depleted regiment was needed to make a battalion.

Thus, the size of the larger units to which a regiment was assigned might not be apparent when reading about battle.

Usually a brigade would have four or five regiments but sometimes as many as eight. A brigadier general commanded a brigade but often was a colonel from one of the regiments until promoted.

Three brigades made up a division, under a major general, or a brigadier until promoted.

Three divisions made a corps, also under a major general. These numbers varied within an army, which might have three corps. Schofield's Army of the Ohio had just one.

Friday, May 13, 1864

Confederate General Joseph Johnston's army was racing to get to Resaca, Georgia ahead of Union General William Sherman's armies. Johnston had to keep Sherman from the Confederacy's source of supply, Atlanta, Georgia. Both armies depended on a railroad that ran from Nashville, Tennessee to Atlanta. Sherman was trying hard to get to Resaca first so he could cut off Johnston's access to the railroad. He had already tried it with a smaller army, the Tennessee, but their commander, General McPherson, found it too risky, especially when Confederate infantry was arriving at Resaca from the south. So now Sherman had sent all he had, leaving behind only part of one corps, the Fourth, under O.O. Howard, who were pushing Johnston's rear.

McPherson had gotten around Johnston by sneaking through Snake Creek Gap, on a narrow road hidden between two long ridges. But this time Johnston learned of Sherman's move and was trying desperately to get to Resaca first. There, in some hills, he had fortifications ready, built during the winter. He had many fortifications ready—all the way to Atlanta. He could not expect that his 60,000 men would beat Sherman's better-supplied 100,000 unless Sherman made a catastrophic mistake somewhere along the line. So he at least needed to slow down Sherman and keep him fully occupied until the November elections in the hope that Union President Lincoln would be defeated, which might mean the Union would end the war. He also was drawing Sherman further and further from his supply and support from Nashville. So, as Johnston got closer to Atlanta, he would be closer to support and Sherman would be more spread out and vulnerable, especially being in enemy territory. That was the game Johnston had to play. If Sherman cut him off at Resaca, the game would be over.

The Plan

Sherman already knew his second attempt to get ahead was failing. So he and his former West Point roommate, General George Thomas, who commanded the largest army, the Cumberland, worked out another plan.

Thomas wrote to Sherman: *In this situation of affairs the enemy must be completely cut off, or compelled to retreat by the various fords southeast of Dalton, across the Connesauga, in which latter event, if General McPherson will merely threaten Resaca with the head of his column, and force a passage across the Oostenaula at Lay's Ferry, and take up a strong position on the hills bordering the railroad southeast of Lay's Ferry, Johnston will be compelled to retreat through, the mountains to Allatoona.*

That is: we must force Johnston off the railroad and into the hills by cutting him off below Resaca.

If Johnston was trapped at Resaca, Sherman could send most of his units to Atlanta while others would hold Johnston under siege or break up his army. That might force Lee to send help. Or Sherman might send help to Grant. So Johnston had to somehow gather up his army at Resaca and then get in front of Sherman.

Sherman wrote back: *Until I hear that Joe Johnston is south of the Oostenaula I would not cross at Lay's. We must first interpose between Dalton and Resaca, threatening the latter all the time.*

Here at Resaca, Sherman did not want to fight where Johnston would be protected by trenches in hills—which gave him a three-to-one advantage—and by a muddy creek on one side and a river on the other.

So he wanted to block Johnston in Resaca on the north while staying hidden below Resaca until Johnston is forced to leave by crossing the river on the south. Then Sherman would cross the river and ambush Johnston above Calhoun and keep him off the railroad. That would leave Johnston nowhere to go—except out of the way.

That might be like trying to corner a wildcat in a cave and then lure him out the only exit. (One does not take on a wildcat in close quarters.) So, as Sherman said, he had to keep his men hidden till the cat came out. But if the cat darted past Calhoun, it would be gone. Who would be quicker? Failure would mean fighting all the way to Atlanta. Cats are notoriously good at distracting their prey, or their predator, and then watching for their chance to pounce, or to slip away, feigning disinterest while they do it.

Sherman telegraphed Halleck, the army chief in Washington: *By the flank movement on Resaca we have forced Johnston to evacuate Dalton, and we are on his flank and rear, but the parallelism of the valleys and mountains does not give us all the advantage of an open country, but I will press him all that is possible.*

Going to Work

McPherson's Army of the Tennessee had entrenched and guarded the gap, waiting for Thomas. Among the first to arrive was General Daniel Butterfield's division of General Joseph Hooker's 20th Corps. It had taken three days. They first had to rebuild and widen the five miles of narrow road before the others, wagon trains and all, could come behind them. The project took *Three men ordered to each tool to push the work vigorously.* So most of Johnston's army were already in the area, but they were too late to plug the gap and stop Thomas.

While the others skirmished in Sugar Valley, Howard's 4th Corps kept close behind the last Rebel units, coming down the road from Dalton to Resaca.

Among the last through Snake Creek Gap was Harker's brigade from General Schofield's Army of Ohio, the smallest Union army. Captain Thrustin, of the 111th Ohio Infantry Regiment, recalls for his comrades their arrival after the fighting at Dalton, to face again the waiting Rebels:

The night before, fifteen miles to the northward we had seen the mountains lit up with the incessant flashes of musketry and cannon. Now, as the darkness settled upon us, we saw the rebel camp fires in our front. Our march from Loudon southward to Rocky Face had been over a country new to us and therefore interesting, and when the day's march had become wearisome it needed only a few notes from fife and drum, of "The Girl I Left Behind Me", to put elasticity into your step, to bring the straggler to his place in ranks, and then while the natives stared with open mouthed wonder, you would break out with

"We are coming from the east, we are coming from the west,
Shouting the battle cry of freedom,
And we'll drive the rebel crew, from the land we love the best,
Shouting the battle cry of freedom.
The Union for ever, hurrah boys, hurrah,
Down with the traitors, and up with the stars,
While we rally round the flag boys, rally once again,
Shouting the battle cry of freedom."

When were you too weary to join in that chorus? Now, as you moved up through the dense woods upon the rebel position, the voice of music was hushed, every one talked in an undertone when it was necessary to talk. Every man felt that there was desperate business on hand, and melody would have rasped the nerves like a neuralgia.

As Schofield and Thomas pressed outward, McPherson pushed ahead to the river.

Bald Hill

Pushing to Resaca itself, McPherson captured a high hill overlooking the town and its bridges. The view drew attention, including from the commander of the Union forces in the west and the one-time commander in the east, who was still looking to regain prestige he lost in the Battle of Chancellorsville.

General Schofield, 23rd Corps: *The first time I ever saw General Sherman and General Hooker together, or got even a suspicion that their personal relations were other than the most satisfactory, was at Resaca. Cox's division had gained possession of some portions of the enemy's outer works, so that from a bald hill just in rear of our line some parts of the main line of defense could be distinctly seen. Upon my informing General Sherman of this, he soon appeared on the ground, accompanied or closely followed by a large number of general and staff officers. Besides Sherman, Thomas, Hooker, and*

Newton, a score of others were there, all eager to see what they could of the now famous stronghold which McPherson had refrained from assaulting. I led them to the hill, on which a few dead trees were still standing, and from which the much-desired view could be obtained. Of course all were on foot, yet they were too numerous not to attract the attention of the enemy. Very soon the sound of musketry in front, then not very heavy, was varied by the sharp explosion of a shell overhead, and fragments of branches of dead trees came falling all around. A general scatteration occurred in all directions save one. Newton and I, who were conversing at the time, quietly stepped aside a few paces out of the line of fire, where we were much safer than we would have been in full retreat, and then turned round to see what had become of our companions. All save two had disappeared, even Thomas having abandoned the field, probably for the first and only time in his life. But still there, on the bald hill, in full view of the hostile artillery, were the two already highly distinguished generals, Sherman and Hooker, both alike famous for supreme courage, striding round the ground, appearing to look at nothing in particular and not conversing with each other, but seeming at least a foot taller than usual, each waiting for the other to lead off in retreat. After quite a long continuance of this little drama, which greatly entertained Newton and me, the two great soldiers, as if by some mysterious impulse,—for they did not speak a word,—simultaneously and slowly strode to the rear, where their horses were held.

Toward the river, Camp Creek passed through a gap and swung close to town where a road from the west crossed a bridge over the creek. Seen from the hill that got so much interest was another hill, across the creek. It was heavily defended, for from there artillery could easily the shell the bridges.

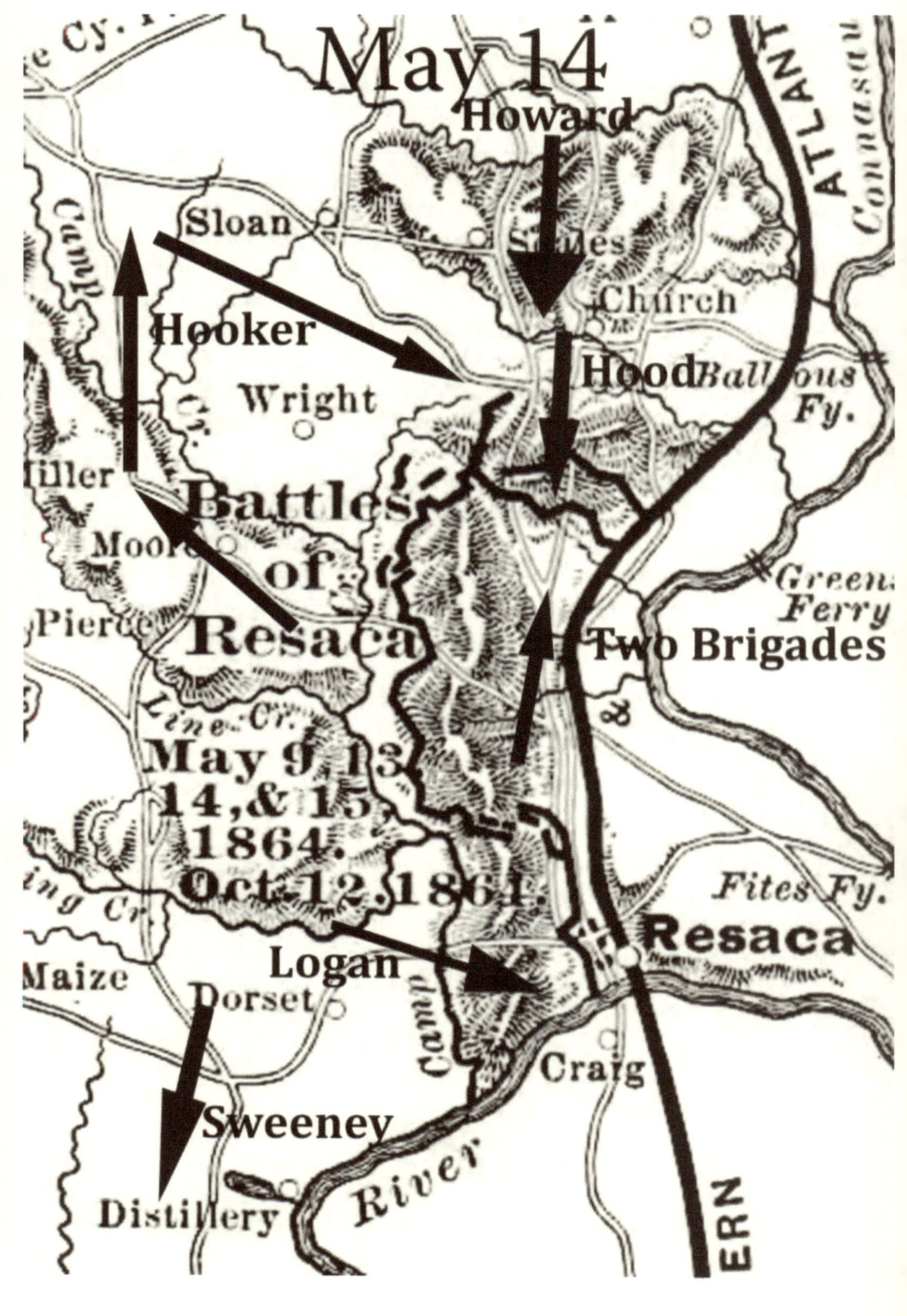

May 14
Howard
Sloan
Hooker
Wright
Church
Hood
Ballous Fy.
Miller
Battles
Moore
of
Green Ferry
Pierce
Resaca
Two Brigades
Line Cr.
May 9, 13,
14, & 15,
1864.
Oct. 12. 1864.
Fites Fy.
Maize
Logan
Resaca
Dorset
Sweeney
Craig
Distillery
River
ATLANTA
Connasau
ERN
Camp
Camp

Saturday, May 14

By now the armies were facing each other along a two-mile front on either side of Camp Creek all the way south to the river. Union forces were in the hills on the west side of the creek. Rebel forces on the east were dug in. Behind the Rebels was the road that ran from Dalton to Resaca and across the river. Union attacks along that line started early.

Pontoons South

Sherman was working on the plan. General Corse was his staff officer coordinating:

Sherman to Corse: *The pontoon instead of going direct to Lay's from the gap, came this way, but it must now be near you. Keep it out of sight till the last moment. Get all things ready under cover for our bridge and make a lodgment by means of all the other boats; there are enough for three bridges. General Sweeny's division is also on its way, and I want it to-day (or to-night will do) across the Oostenaula in a strong defensive position out from the river about a mile on the best ground that can be found, and roads cut to the bridges. As soon as one bridge is done, the other should also be made there, if possible. I will send more infantry if necessary.*

While Sherman worked the boats south, Thomas worked to squeeze the Rebels into their works across Camp Creek.

Butterfield Busy

Butterfield's division was just north of McPherson's Army.

Sgt. Major Fleharty, 102nd Ill, Ward's 1st Brigade: *Early in the morning a dash forward to Camp Creek was made. Being then mere novices in the art of warfare, many of the men took up positions where they were quite at the mercy of the enemy and were compelled to remain behind stumps and trees all day an attempt to escape being equivalent to certain death. It was an exciting day on the skirmish line; firing commenced at daylight, and was kept, up until dark.*

At one time the enemy endeavored to flank the line, and Capt. left and drove the enemy back. Meanwhile there was heavier work on the left. The skirmishing had been lively in that direction all the forenoon, but at 2 o'clock p.m. the firing became terrific. There was a perpetual roll of musketry, and the deep bass of the artillery reverberated grandly through the woods and was echoed back by the surrounding hills. At that time we were ordered forward, and the moment we appeared on the little elevation in front of the ravine, the rebel sharpshooters sent their balls whistling around us, killing one man instantly and wounding three. Having proceeded a short distance, we were ordered to halt and lie down. The object doubtless was to make a feint of attacking, in order to divert the attention of the enemy from the left. No further advance was attempted, and we remained in that position until late in the evening, listening occasionally to the whizzing of bullets above our heads, but more deeply interested in the fierce conflict on our left. The sound at times would run along the line towards us, until it would seem that our Corps must soon, also, become engaged, then it would recede, and there would be a lull, like the lulling of the winds in a winter storm. Sometimes it would seem that our men were driving the rebels, and again it appeared that the battle was going against us. O! how terrible the suspense of waiting at such a time for victory, while contemplating the possibility of disaster! The sound of the battle at its height could only be compared in my mind to the work of a storm, breaking and crushing to the ground, ten thousand dead trees every instant, amid the roll of heaven's artillery. A battery about fifty yards to the left of our regiment was kept busy throwing shot and shell into the rebel lines, but the guns of the enemy were engaged where the contest raged more fiercely, and they paid no attention to this battery.

That firing in the afternoon we will find out about shortly.

Robert Hale Strong, of the 105th Illinois: *Our brigade [Harrison's] was ordered to the right flank to support the troops engaged in fighting there. I distinctly remember how plain we could hear the whole business: the roar of the artillery, the crack of musketry, the cheers of the Yankees and the yells of the Johnnies. Through it all, we were lying in a thick wood and could see nothing. When we would hear the Yankees cheer, our hearts would almost stop beating. Then would come the roar of Rebel cannon, and as our boys were beaten back the Rebs would nearly split their throats yelling. We lay there in a fever of impatience until our turn came.*

The plan at this point was for Hooker to follow Dodge across the river at Lay's Ferry when Johnston crossed. His other two divisions were in reserve.

Winslow Homer's drawing shows a line of infantry in the usual two ranks, elbow to elbow, ramrods waving, all facing front, but few in firing posture, illustrating the need for skill and discipline to fight in the Civil War. (Courtesy of Library of Congress.)

Safety in Numbers

Firing one shot left an infantry soldier completely defenseless while he went through several steps to prepare another shot. So infantry was massed in line elbow to elbow to hold off a like adversary. It was a duel. Numbers counted—along with skill at reloading, which had to be fast. It is hard not to fumble while you are being shot at and your comrades are falling around you, bloody and screaming.

Such fights were a trap if the adversary could keep you busy facing one way while others tried to get around behind you. On your flank was even more deadly. Firing along the line at an angle (enfilading) was a sure shot and you cannot just turn around and shoot back.

But how do you rapidly move and re-arrange lines of hundreds of men in these conditions? Colonels and generals had to learn many tactics and drill with their men over and over. How do you swing a line through a gate? The more they learned and drilled, the more options they had to work with in the heat of battle when situations were not according to plan—which is usually after the first shot.

Then there is communication. Over the whole field of battle, ranging over creeks and mud, forest and hill, and unmarked roads full of wagons and men, how do commanders know what is happening and what they are expected to do—where to send their units? Just the sound of cannon and musket echoing in the hills has misdirected many a plan. Only scribbled notes carried on foot or horseback was reliable. Generals had large staffs for that purpose—to keep them informed and to send orders. Time stood still, waiting while battle raged. Sometimes multiple couriers were sent through the storm and earned medals because, being prized targets, they often did not return.

At the Head of Camp Creek

Schofield's army was in the northern end of the Union line facing the creek. One of his generals, Judah, was so anxious he sent his division ahead of other units on the line. Thrustin tells us what happened that afternoon when they tried to attack across a muddy valley where the enemy could easily shell them from a distance:

On the morning of the 14th of May, 1864, we were under orders to attack the rebel position in our front. Between our skirmishers and the rebel entrenchments upon a course nearly southward, Camp Creek ran on its way to the Oostanaula. About sunrise I rode to the top of the ridge, where our skirmishers were posted, and delivered orders to be followed during the attack, by the officer in command. Taking a rifle from one of our men, I fired several times, at working parties of the Confederates, who were just finishing their intrenchments. The object was to determine the distance between the lines. At each discharge of my gun the commotion among the enemy indicated that the bullet reached them. I returned and reported to Colonel Bond that the ridge was a commanding position for our artillery, and ought to be occupied before the charge was made. At his request I rode to General Haskell's headquarters and repeated the report to him. With an indifferent manner he replied that probably General Judah would attend to the matter, and I then returned and reported his reply.

Some hours afterward our lines were massed upon the ridge overlooking the rebel intrenchments, and within long musket range, and without artillery support we moved to the attack. As soon as we uncovered from the woods we were saluted with a storm of shell, followed by grape, canister and musket balls; we dashed forward and jumped into the creek hoping to obtain shelter from the dreadful fire. From the channel of the creek we delivered our fire, but when the men set their guns on the ground to push home the next cartridge, the guns were forced into the yielding mud, covering the tubes with water so that they would not discharge. In a few moments most of the guns were disabled. Efforts were made to advance, and here and there along the line, soldiers, single or in groups, rushed forward to the apparent cover of stumps or trees, but our advance had placed us under an enfilading fire, which searched out every corner of the field.

At length we were ordered to return to the top of the ridge, where we reformed our lines, and again advanced to the charge, only adding to our casualties without the power to do the enemy any injury. General Judah, then commanding our division, came forward to our line on foot, and finding it impossible to carry the works, ordered us to retreat.

We had been made the victims of an inexcusable blunder. The ridge from which we charged was much higher than the opposite ridge occupied by the enemy; and had our artillery been placed upon it, could have silenced the rebel guns, covered our charge, and probably, given us victory instead of defeat. General Judah stated that he had sent out his staff officers in the morning to inspect the position, and they reported that the ridge was inaccessible to artillery, and hence no effort was made to get the guns in position. Within a half-hour after the disaster, the artillery was posted on the hill, but the charging columns lay in broken fragments in the valley.

A General of Division who does not personally inspect the field of a contemplated battle, and look critically over every point of advantage for his men, which the topography affords, is not fit to command troops.

Our regiment went into that action with over five hundred muskets, and came out of it so crippled that we were able to muster only 107 guns when we rallied on the ridge.

The upturned faces down the hill side, in the valley, and the bodies floating in the muddy water of the creek accounted for some of them. The ambulances and stretcher-bearers reported others. There were some who in the confusion of the charge and counter charge had been swept off the field by the retreat of other commands.

Judah was soon removed from command and Harker replaced him.

Shelling from Bald Hill

Meantime, closer to the river, from the bald hill he'd captured yesterday, Logan's Corps was shelling the defenders at Camp Creek, especially that hill on the other side, closer to the bridges. If Sherman got that hill, he would threaten Johnston's ability to get out of Resaca.

So now, Saturday afternoon, May 14, 1864, Johnston knew time was short. He had saved his army by gathering them in these hills, where one man could hold off three, until he found a way to get by Sherman. He needed that railroad for supplies: ammunition and food. To save his army he needed to cross the river before Sherman. That was his problem.

But his army was still strung out on the road from Dalton—Hood was not in yet.

Hood Arrives

Following Hood's Corps from Dalton was the last of Sherman's forces, two divisions, Wood's and Stanley's, under General Howard. The last Confederate units had marched all night Friday and arrived in the morning. Hood kept Clack's 3rd Tennessee skirmishing to slow down Wood and Stanley. Early that afternoon, Stanley's division arrived on a parallel road and waited for Wood's division to arrive on the main road.

Colonel Day, 101st Ohio, Cruft's brigade: *Our Corps halted ... within a mile of the Confederate main works. ... The 101st was ordered forward as skirmishers, as indeed it had been both that day and the day before, every time we came in contact with the enemy. At least half a dozen times on the march the column had been halted, and the 101st passed to the front, until it became a common saying among the boys of the other regiments: The rebs are in front; there goes the 101st forward. The skirmishing here was pressed with such vigor over the rough, wooded sides of the broken ridge that it assumed almost the proportions of battle. The enemy was steadily driven back toward their main line.*

Then they began serious work. Wood's three brigades worked their way south on the right side of the road, to connect with Schofield. They were skirmishing with Rebels who were digging in on the hills on the left side.

One of Wood's brigades, Hazen's, faced a line along a ridge directly across the road:

The advance was a difficult one, through thick woods and tangled undergrowth. The skirmishers drove those of the enemy before them for about three miles, when Colonel Payne, who had relieved Colonel Foy in the front, drove a Rebel line handsomely across a cornfield into their works beyond, and gained a strong position within two hundred yards of their intrenchments. His line was here exposed to an enfilading fire from a battery, but Colonel Kimberly's battalion, charging across the field and forming nearly at right angles with Colonel Payne's, soon silenced it, and held the position within seventy-five yards of the enemy's main line. The cannoneers were driven away from their guns, and only succeeded in recovering them after dark.

Stanley spread out across the road and over a hill on the left. Cavalry had been helping skirmish with the last of the Rebels till Stanley arrived. Then they left to watch the east side of Johnston's line, leaving Stanley alone. Wood was on the right of the road and was linking with Schofield. But nobody was coming behind Stanley and nobody was on his left, between him and the railroad.

Sherman was aware of the gap and wanted it closed.

Saving Simonson's Battery May 14
Approximate Movements
Showing regiments whose positions were given.

RG Miller

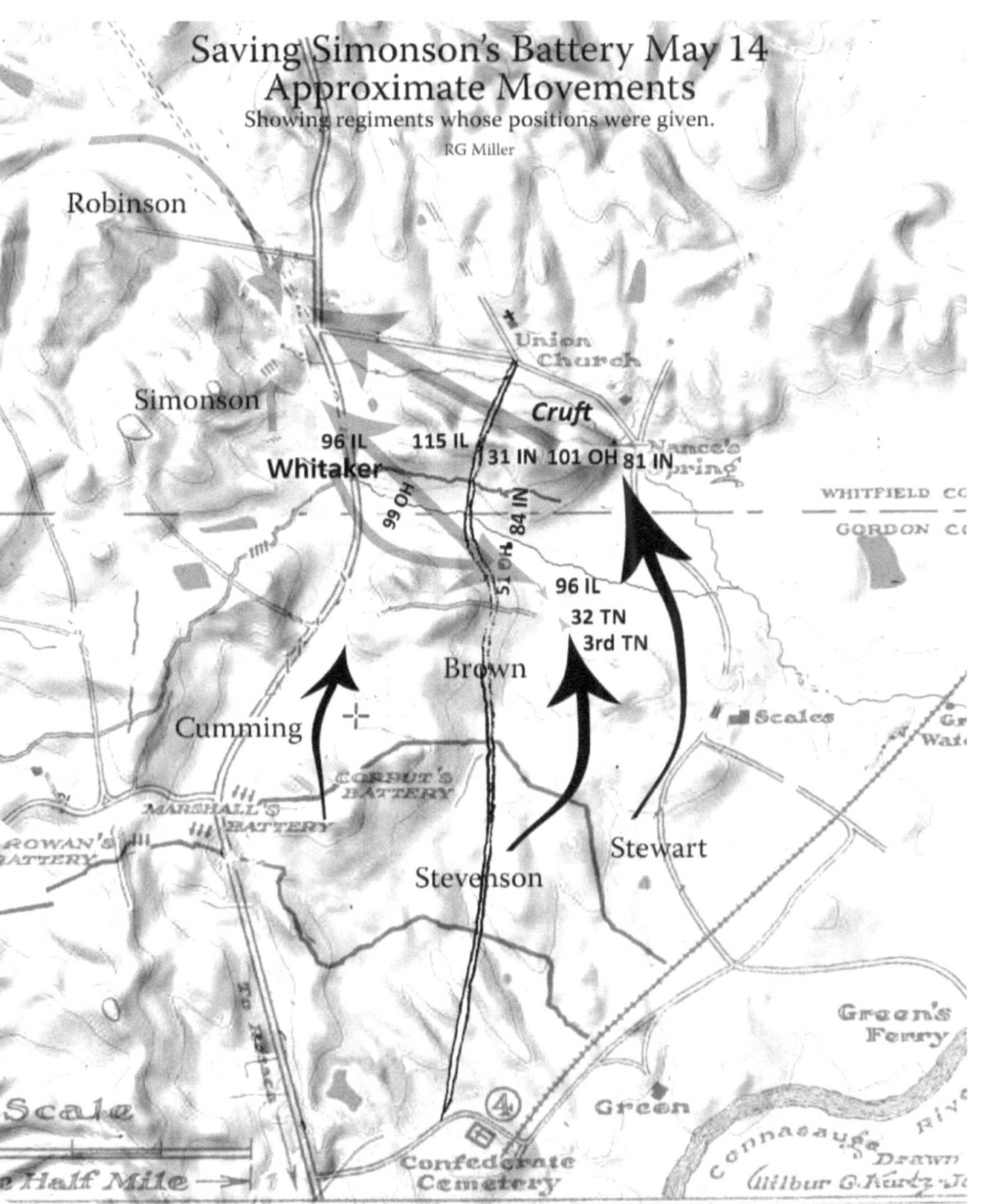

Waiting in Those Hills

Somewhere, unseen in those trees on the hills on the other side of that field, was the waiting enemy. Along the road for two miles south they were dug in on the hills, clear to the town of Resaca at the Oostanaula River—all of Johnston's 60,000 facing all of Sherman's 100,000.

So, there on the north end, Stanley's men stood looking across a little plain at the trees in the hills while the rest of Sherman's and Johnston's forces were busy fighting. Artillery was dueling.

Find Them

Stanley can't just stand there. He has to deploy before the Rebels decide to turn on him. But he does not know where their well-hidden line is. The only way to find out is to get shot at.

Often in war a regiment is so well trained, experienced, and commanded that they keep getting the harder jobs. That is Colonel Champion's 96th Illinois, of Whitaker's brigade. They spread out and went forward, carefully. This is called developing the enemy position by skirmishing. Nerve-wracking work. Their top enlisted man, Sergeant Major Partridge, tells us how they found the Rebel line.

Partridge, 96th Ill Whitaker's 2nd Brigade: *The Fourth Corps was on the extreme left of the general army, the First Division, to which the Ninety-sixth was attached, was the left of the Corps, and for the time being Whittaker's was the left Brigade of the Division. It required most of the forenoon to move the Corps into place and connect the lines with those of the Twenty-third Corps, on the right. During this period comparative quiet reigned upon the extreme left, but farther to the right, where the troops were swinging forward to develop the enemy's position, there was a volume of firing whose magnitude indicated that a battle was in progress. At a little after two o'clock the left was ordered forward. Promptly the line moved out, Companies A and B deployed as skirmishers. [Company B was normally on the left end of the regiment and Company A was normally on the right.] Beyond the open field mentioned was a wooded ridge, from which came shots to indicate that it was held by the enemy. The advance to this ridge was resisted, but not with such force as to compel a charge. As the skirmishers neared its top they were greeted with a hot fire, indicating that the enemy were in heavy force a little farther on. As it proved the advancing line was not parallel to the enemy's works, the left of Company B being much nearer than the right of Company A. This fact was not at once appreciated, and Captain Vincent, the ranking officer and hence the commanding officer of the line, repeatedly called out, as the men halted, 'Forward on the left! Forward on the left!' Captain Gilmore repeated the order to his men, and most gallantly they responded, going at a charge, driving the enemy's skirmishers from their positions and halting only when the main works of the Rebels were in plain view and a volley warned them that to go farther would be extremely perilous. In this advance Herman Hoogstraat, of Company B, was killed by one of the Rebel skirmishers, the latter quickly paying the penalty, for before the smoke from his musket had cleared away, Mack McMillen's trusty rifle rang out its response, and when the line advanced the Rebel was found dead where he had fallen. John Bininger, of Company A, was the target of the Rebels for a time, they getting range of the old stump behind which he had taken shelter and filling it full of holes. A bad bruise to his shoulder, a severely scratched face and a considerable amount of bark and dirt in his eyes constituted his inventory of physical damages. It being demonstrated that the left was as far advanced as was practicable, the right was swung around to conform and the reserves moved up until they stood confronting a field, a half mile in width. This field was broken with hills and seamed with gullies, with a timbered ridge at the left.*

Whitaker saw the hill he faced was an "admirable position for artillery". Indeed, the Rebs were busy strengthening it. He was actually preparing to attack with his one brigade when Stanley came by and stopped it.

Colonel Champion's 96th Illinois had done their job. Stanley positioned Captain Peter Simonson's 5th Indiana Battery of six guns on the right of the road to shell the Rebels on the other side of that valley.

Stanley placed Cruft's and Whitaker's brigades across a hill on the left and across the road on their right, connecting with Grose's brigade, which connected with Wood's division. They looked south, facing those trees across the field. Those on the east end saw nothing but the railroad in the distance. No support was behind them. The end of the line was alone, in the air as they say.

Johnston Shifts

Johnston, in effect, had drawn Sherman's forces in close, like a vacuum, leaving empty space behind them. There was that inviting gap between Cruft and the railroad. Could he now turn on Sherman and get behind him? Johnston ordered two brigades sent north to help Hood.

That move weakened Confederate General Polk's line where Logan's division had been fighting all day and shelling Polk's line from Bald Hill.

Logan Pounces

Captain Tremain, Butterfield's Staff: *While the enemy had been thoroughly occupied in repelling Schofield's advance and afterwards attacking him in force, McPherson boldly assailed the enemy's extreme left in front of Resaca. The artillery opened along the whole line, and under its cover and a heavy skirmish fire Logan's corps crossed Camp Creek, and by a skillful and gallant charge, drove the enemy from the commanding hills in our front, and secured such a position across the creek as subjected a portion of the enemy's works to our destructive enfilading fire. Thus, while at the close of the afternoon action, the lines of both armies at the left remained substantially in the same positions, on the extreme right Logan with his veterans had gained a most decided advantage.*

Now Polk had barely any distance between his line and the railroad where he faced Logan's artillery.

Hood Pops Out

Like a gopher whacked at one entrance, Johnston had Hood pop out at the other—more like an angry lion than a groundhog.

Simonson and others were bothering Hood with their artillery. Scouts noticed Hood was forming his divisions, preparing for attack. That empty space between Cruft and the railroad was an open invitation.

Colonel Day, 101st Ohio, Crufts brigade: *So imminent was the danger at this point, and to our Brigade especially, that to avoid capture, our batteries, under Captain Simonson, were withdrawn and so placed as to rake our present position after we should be driven back.*

That one move, from an offensive to a defensive position, would save Stanley's division and buy time to plug the gap.

Stanley immediately sent for help. Hooker's corps was down near Resaca with two divisions in reserve. Thomas ordered them north to help Stanley. Hooker got them started on the backroads to the north and then rode ahead himself.

Stanley ordered Whitaker's brigade back and around the nose of that hill. Forward again went Colonel Champion's 96th Illinois, toward the east side of the hill, where Stewart's Division was hidden in the trees. As he got closer, Champion sent two companies probing the brush. They could not see anything—till they came face-to-face with skirmishers emerging from the woods.

Hooker arrived and told Simonson he would get more ammunition and to hold on till Williams' division got there. Simonson told his men *Our big time has come.* What was coming was Brown's Brigade, of Stevenson's Division, led by the 3rd Tennessee, heading straight for Simonson's battery. Brown ran right over Whitaker's men, who had to run for their lives toward the battery. Stewart's Division was coming too. They split and hit Cruft's hill on three sides. One of Cruft's regiments had been firing so fast at the Rebels that they stuck their ramrods into the ground, to load faster. Those were left behind as they fled toward the battery.

All Simonson could do was fire over the head of Whitaker's men till they got past him. Then he put muzzles down and opened up, staggering Brown. As Cruft's men arrived, Simonson turned his guns left on the Rebels that came after them. Robinson was coming and could see the action from a ridge. Whitaker and Cruft frantically gathered aside Simonson and tried to defend. Simonson's men were firing at about 4 rounds a minute, risking getting the barrels so hot the metal would expand and the guns could not be loaded.

Holm, Simonson's 5th Indiana Battery: *Pandemonium reigned for about fifteen minutes, when suddenly there came from somewhere in the rear close by the command, 'c-e-a-s-e f-i-r-ing, lie down'. This was repeated, and the voice was recognized as that of Captain Simonson. It was but a moment till not a man of the Battery could be seen except as he lay upon the ground in the place where he stood while in action. Hooker had redeemed his promise—two lines of infantry with fixed bayonets came charging through the battery and out across the valley in close pursuit of the residue of fleeing Confederates.*

It was Robinson's brigade.

Illinois Adjutant General History of 101st Ill: *The 101st [Illinois] was ordered to take a hill in front of them, occupied by the enemy, which they did in so gallant a style as to win the admiration of General Joe Hooker, who cheered the troops, with the encouraging shout of: 'Go in, my Illinois boys!'*

Benton, Band, 150th NY Ruger's 2nd Brigade: *'Blow cease firing!' The voice was of Gen. A. S. Williams, old Pop Williams, as the boys affectionately referred to him among themselves, and the order was addressed to the brigade bugler, Stevenson, who, as it happened, was a member of our regiment. Stevenson had been as intensely interested as the others in the drama before us, and he afterward told me that it was the only time he was ever ordered to blow 'Cease firing'. Now, with the suddenness of the order he could not remember the signal, but he clapped the bugle to his lips and blew something; and the firing ceased. The signal had not been needed, for the men saw that the enemy had retreated from their front, and they stopped firing without regard to that uncertain sound from Stevenson's instrument.*

It was "Fighting Joe" Hooker's forte: attack. He was an excellent leader, but his ability to grasp overall battlefield conditions and work out strategy on the fly, lacking at Chancellorsville, was still in doubt.

Prior Battles Mentioned Herein

September, 1862 Louisville: After being driven out of Kentucky and Tennessee, the Rebel army came back under Bragg and almost reached Louisville. Raw volunteer regiments on the way forced Bragg to withdraw.

October 8, 1862 Perryville, Kentucky: Bragg's Rebel army withdrew, moving south.

December 31, 1862-January 3, 1863 Stones River, Tennessee: Fought to a draw by Rosecrans, Bragg wintered at Tullahoma while Rosecrans prepared to chase him back to Georgia.

May 1-4, 1863 Chancellorsville: Hooker took over the Army of the Potomac and thought he had Lee cornered. But Stonewall Jackson flanked Howard, who Hooker had warned, after a night march. Hooker abandoned the fight.

July 3, 1863 Gettysburg: Hooker was stalking Lee's invasion of Pennsylvania but resigned. Defeated, Lee withdrew to Virginia.

July 4, 1863 Vicksburg: Grant, with Sherman and McPherson, captured the last Rebel hold on Mississippi after a long campaign.

September 19-20, 1863 Chickamauga: Thomas and Rosecrans invaded Georgia after driving Bragg's army out of Kentucky and Tennessee. Hood, under Longstreet, broke the Union line and Rosecrans' half of the army fled leaving Thomas to earn the title "Rock of Chickamauga" by fighting until dark and then retreating to Chattanooga, there to be under siege by Bragg.

November 23-25, 1863 Chattanooga: Hooker fought off a night attack at Wauhatchie after helping Grant reach Thomas at Chattanooga. Then Hooker took Lookout Mountain, as a demonstration, the day before Thomas' brigades stormed Missionary Ridge to aid Sherman's effort on the north end, driving Bragg to winter quarters at Dalton, where he was replaced by Johnston.

Ambition

This was not the first time General Williams was taken out of position to rescue a battery. At Gettysburg his division was called out of its position at night and the Rebs took it while he was gone. Another General, Geary, was supposed to be there but had gotten lost on the road. Yet Geary took full credit for saving the line that Williams' men had to recover.

Now, at Resaca, Geary's division followed Williams north. Both camped for the night north of that little plain.

Though both had led divisions for some time, Geary and Williams were still brigadier generals. On occasion, Williams led corps and did so effectively. Then, in October, when Williams was to take his division to the front at Chattanooga and Geary was to protect the railroad, Geary complained about Williams getting all the opportunities for glory. So he got sent instead and promptly lost his son in the Battle of Wauhatchie. In grief and fury, he sent his men up Lookout Mountain.

Brig. Gen. John Geary, 2nd Division, 20th Corps: *I have been like a destroying angel ever since, no height has been too bold, no valley too deep, no fastness too stormy, that I did not solicit to be permitted to storm. Permission was granted, and with the assistance of bold hearts and willing hands, I have been the instrument of Almighty God, of carrying terror and terrible destruction wherever it has pleased God to direct my footsteps. Under such impulses I stormed, what was considered the impassible and inaccessible heights of Lookout Mountain, I captured it, turned the right flank of Bragg's army and drove him from his position. This feat will be celebrated until time shall be no more.*

He was looking for more opportunities.

The Results of the Day

Now, two of Hooker's three divisions, Williams' and Geary's, were north. Major General Dan Butterfield, Hooker's long-time Chief of Staff, who outranked them, was still across from Camp Creek.

McPherson could easily shell Resaca's bridges.

Johnston, alerted that Sweeny had crossed at Lay's Ferry, ordered Hood to evacuate the hill that Whitaker so admired, leaving it vacant. Then Sweeny was driven back, an admirable (unintended) feint—if used to advantage.

Sherman seemed to realize that Johnston was onto his game when he telegraphed Washington: *Sherman to Halleck: May 14 8 pm: We have had hard fighting all day. Johnston purely on the defensive. The place has small detached redoubts, and in immense amount of rifle trenches. We have close [sic]the enemy well in, gaining ground slowly but securely all day. The country is very rough and woody. I will renew the attack at all points to-morrow, and continue till Johnston retreats, and then shall follow.*

Johnston immediately ordered a pontoon bridge built on the Oostenaula upstream from Resaca, gaining another way to cross if Sherman kept him from using the other bridges.

Also waiting for the morrow, those who would be engaged with the remains of the day for the rest of the campaign:

Mrs. Porter, Sanitary Commission, May 14: *Mrs. Bickerdyke left on the 10th for Chattanooga. I followed on Wednesday. ... I wish I could give you clear description of our mule train. A long solemn train of mule teams! most of them looking as if dragging heavily, and many making a mighty effort to take their last load to the scene of strife. Can you imagine such a train? reaching all the way from Ringgold to Sugar Creek, a distance of twenty five miles. Such a train almost literally filled the way with supplies to our army to-day. The supplies are to go by railroad soon, and the mules which are falling on the right hand and on the left, from over-work, poor fare and exhaustion will be relieved. ... We reached Sugar Creek*

What would have happened to Bickerdyke and Porter had Hood's
turning attempt been successful, had he broken out into Sugar
Valley behind Schofield and Howard? That train of wagons could
have been destroyed and left to block the gap. The railroad being
blocked also, Sherman would be out of supplies and might even be
isolated.

Butterfield's division, after skirmishing all day across Camp Creek,
got some relief:

Sergeant Major Fleharty, of the 102nd Illinois, Ward's 1st Brigade:
*Towards evening the sounds of battle died away, and finally
dwindled down to the irregular firing of the skirmishers. At dusk we
retired to our position in the ravine. The regiment had lost during
the day three men killed, and nineteen wounded. Late at night the
camp was hushed in repose, and beneath the lovely foliage of the
trees we slept sweetly but ere we slept, we looked up through our
leafy covering to the bright stars that twinkled so peacefully in the
calm blue sky, and thought of other and distant skies of peace of
those far away, as dear to us as life and thought of the morrow.*

While they rested, Hooker made plans.

May 15
ATLANT
Connasau
Camp
Sloan
Scales
Butterfield
Church
Williams
Wright
Ballous Fy.
Geary
Hood
Tiller
Battles
Moore
of
Green Ferry
Pierce
Resaca
Line Cr.
May 9, 13,
14, & 15,
1864.
Oct. 12, 1864.
Fites Fy.
Maize
Resaca
Dorset
Camp
Hood
Craig
Bragg
Distillery
River
Polk
ERN

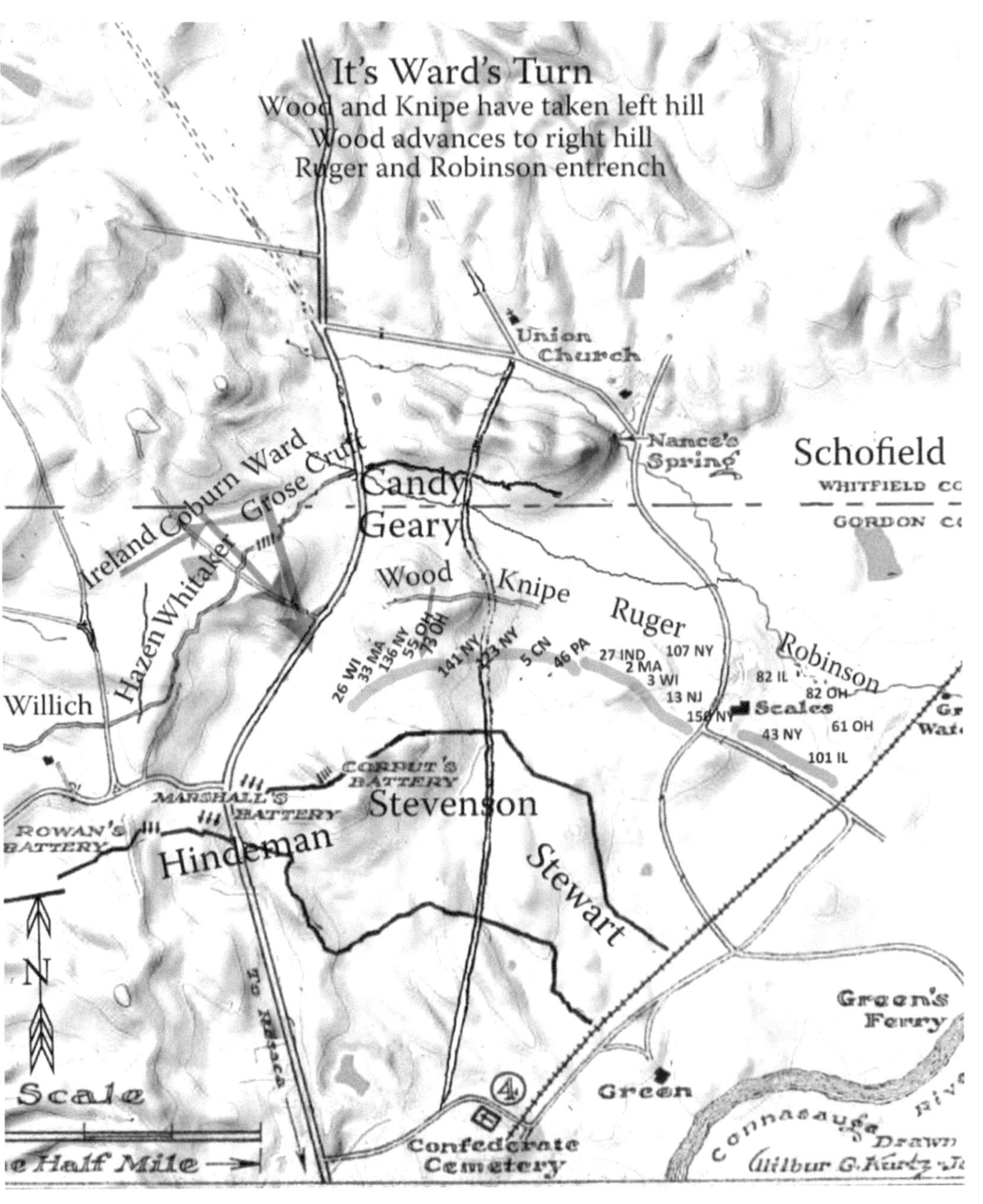

R.G. Miller's adaptation of Wilbur Kurtz' map of trenches.

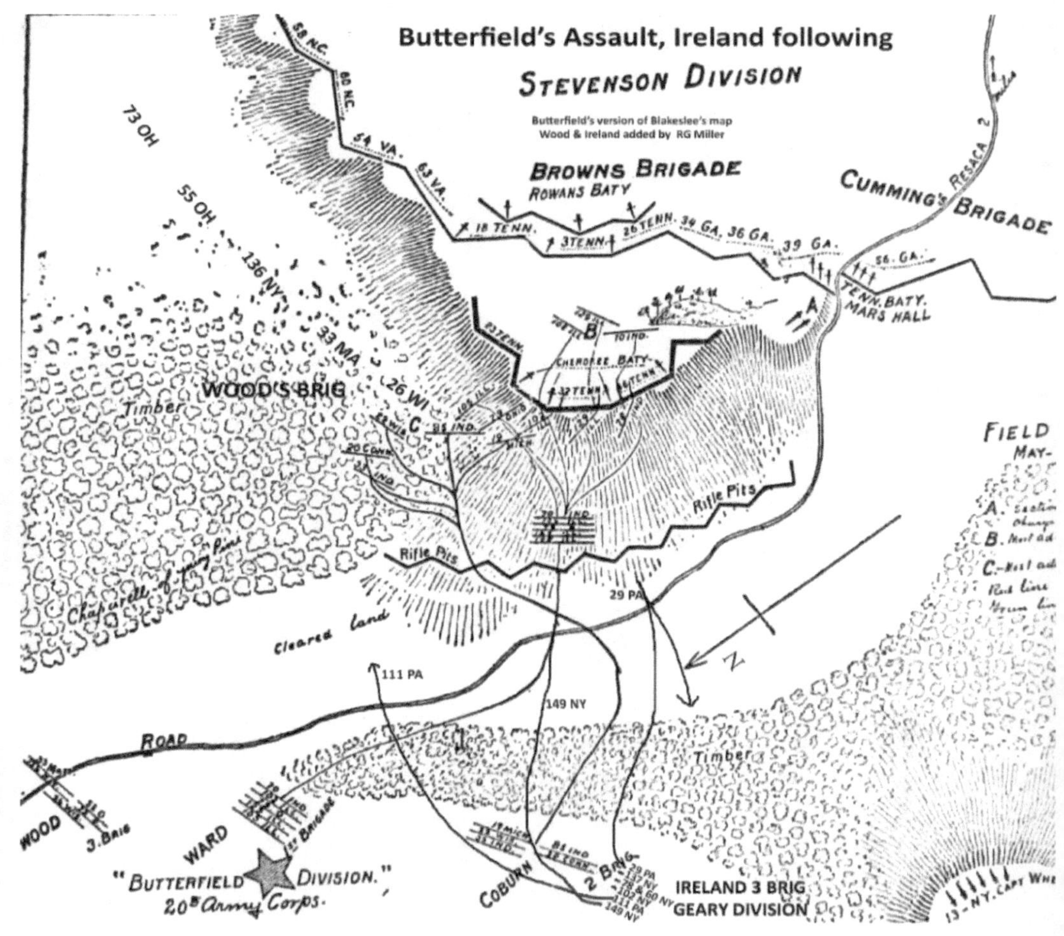

Butterfield's version of the map G.H. Blakeslee drew immediately after the battle. Wood and Ireland added by R. G. Miller.

SUNDAY, MAY 15

I want to hear the sound of those guns coming down upon Resaca.
–Sherman

Opportunity

Hooker to Sherman, 12:30 am: *I reached the left in season to prevent the enemy turning it. … Had any considerable portion of my corps been in position I would have followed up the success.*

To do it effectually in the morning, in my judgment, the advance should be on two lines, one along the line of railroad, the other along the Dalton and Resaca highway. All the troops should be in position by daylight.

Sherman took him up on it. He immediately told Thomas to order Butterfield north and ordered other rearrangements on the line.

Sherman to Thomas, Midnight: General Hooker has just been here …. Order Hooker and Howard to attack in the morning directly south down upon Resaca. This change should be ordered at once and completed by daylight.

And so:

Dawn

Sergeant Major Fleharty, 102nd Illinois, Ward's 1st Brigade: *The morning of Sunday, May 15, 1864, dawned luridly upon us. The smoke of innumerable camp fires had enveloped hill and valley in a hazy mantle. At six o'clock we were ordered to move around to the left of the 14th Army Corps. Quietly we marched back over the hill, and through the shadowy forest, almost feeling the death-like stillness of that memorable Sabbath morning. And how like entering the valley of the shadow of death, seemed our march down through the smoky atmosphere into the deep valley, and around to our new position confronting the enemy. Our Division had been selected for the desperate work of charging a rebel battery, which was supported by a strong force of the enemy behind entrenchments. The ulterior object was to break the enemy's line at that point, and thereby cut the rebel army in twain.*

Did Hooker's plan change between midnight and dawn? From attacking along the railroad and down the road upon Resaca, as Sherman put it, to cut the Rebel army in twain. That is, to cut their line in two parts at the angle. Hooker wanted something that was right behind that line, the same thing Whitaker had wanted.

Case, 129th Ill Ward's 1st Brigade: *Early on the morning of the 15th the brigade was relieved, and the entire division moved from their position (the center) to the extreme left of the line of battle. While on the march I was notified that our brigade was ordered to charge and carry at the point of the bayonet the fort and rifle-pits of the enemy, supported by the Second and Third Brigades of the Third Division.*

The preferred form of attack is persuasion with bullets and shells fired from a distance. Bayonets mean assault, up close and personal: fight to the death.

Butterfield's men are to wield the bayonets.

Yet, in his 5 am orders for the day, Sherman cautioned:

The other two corps, Hooker's and Howard's, will make a steady and strong attack on the enemy along down the ridge between Camp Creek and the Connesauga toward Resaca, but will not assault fortified positions unless sure of success.

Was he yet aware of Hooker's intent? Did Hooker think he had to break the line at the angle to get to the ridge along Camp Creek, instead of bypassing those guns?

Enthusiasm was not overwhelming.

Lt. Col. Merrill, 70th Indiana Ward's 1st Brigade: *On the morning of May fifteenth the regiment was relieved and marched to the left several miles, and as it was Sunday saw men of other organizations engaged in religious services. As the report gained credence that a charge was to be made on the enemy's works, some humorous semisolemn remarks were made by men who were not frequent listeners to the Chaplain's sermons, as to the desirability of halting and spending the day in devotional exercises.*

Sherman has given Hooker the lead. Military protocol being strict in battle, by necessity, Thomas and Howard will defer, as must Schofield. At the angle, it is now Hooker's show and he has the starring role. To the men, the coming assault hangs like an oppressive cloud, while for Hooker it is an opportunity.

Early Preparations

As Butterfield headed north, preliminaries started. Sherman ordered shelling all along the Rebel line, to keep them from attacking him and to prevent moving troops north or south. And to hinder communication.

Sweeny Crosses Again

Sweeny's brigade at Lay's Ferry got an early start:

Corse to Sherman, May 15, morning: *He [Sweeny] sent a party over this morning about daylight and brought over the wounded left there last night, and the officers reported they could see nothing. Upon this information he endeavored to cross his command, when the enemy appeared in strong force. He is now making efforts to push over some troops in the boats under cover of banks lined with skirmishers. Colonel Bane, with two regiments of infantry and a battery of artillery, was sent last night to Calhoun Ferry, and this morning directed to open and make all demonstration possible. General Sweeny will make every effort to get a bridge over. An officer has just reported that we have got two boat-loads over, and the rest of Colonel Rice's brigade is crossing rapidly as possible in a place about one mile distant from where the pontoon boats were launched (and which is a dangerous place now, the enemy having discovered our object).*

Scouting

On the north end, about 7 am, Geary's scouts found only Union and Rebel cavalry watching each other on the other side of the railroad. Someone else went up the hill and found Sherman had not taken it during the night.

Open for Occupation

CJH, Brown's Brigade, Stevenson's Division, CSA: *Sunday morning, at an early hour, we were again ordered forward to take position on the eminence on our front, which we supposed was occupied by the enemy, but our skirmishers moved forward without interruption, and we were soon heavily engaged in throwing up hasty breastworks of logs, chincky, and whatever came to hand.*

Wesley Connor, private, Cherokee Artillery, CSA: *Sunday May 15, 1864 8h A.M. Moved to the ridge on the right of the Resaca road, one and a half miles from R. The position we hold was taken from the Yankees by Gen. Stevenson late yesterday afternoon.*

Wes Connor was a gunner in Max Van Der Corput's Cherokee Battery. They had been paroled after surrendering at Vicksburg last July. Here they were again with four new guns from an Augusta foundry and had already used them at Lookout Mountain in November. After Hooker drove them off Lookout, they moved over to Missionary Ridge and helped hold off Sherman's attacks—aided by infantry that Hooker had also driven off Lookout. Now they'd face Hooker again at the angle at Resaca, flying the same flag flown at Vicksburg—Corput had smuggled it out in his saddle blanket.

The Meeting

About 9 A.M. Hooker's corps was forming up, awaiting orders, and the generals had a meeting.

Cook, Asst. Surgeon, 150th NY Ruger 2nd Brigade: *All was as quiet and serene as a Sabbath morning should be. About 9 A.M. it began to be evident that the different corps commanders were in consultation and had selected a little grove just by our camp for the place of consultation. I forget now, how many generals we saw there, but with their several staffs and body guards there was several acres of them; perhaps acres would be a better way to judge of them. First, and I believe the greatest general of all, was Joe Hooker. Then came two riding side by side with but two arms and two legs between them, General Sickles with but one leg, and General Howard with but one arm, and following came Generals Thomas, Schofield, McPherson, Butterfield, Logan and Sherman. These are all the major generals I remember now, but there were a host more of brigadier generals, in fact, too numerous to mention ... Well, the consultation broke up about 11 a.m. and the different generals and their followers whirled away, leaving us again alone in our glory.*

In such a game of miles-apart moves, commanders must be aware of what the others are to do. What did they decide? What were their orders? Events will make us wonder. Here are instructions Sherman sent sometime during the morning:

Sherman to Thomas: *I have just visited McPherson's line. He occupies a ridge in front of Camp Creek, seemingly within range of the bridge, and the line is pretty well fortified already. McPherson is preparing batteries to advantage guns on his right front (extreme). The guns on Bald Hill enfilade the road into Resaca, which passes around the point of the hill ... Now you have Howard's and Hooker's corps beyond Camp Creek looking south, with Schofield, as it were, in reserve, and the less time we give the enemy to fortify the better. I want to hear the sound of that line advancing directly down the road on Resaca till it comes within range of the forts. Whilst this advance is being made McPherson's guns will make the bridge and vicinity too hot for the passage of troops. I am very anxious this advance should be made today, that we may secure a line whose left rests on the Connesauga.*

That last sentence tells us the prime objective of Hooker's advance, above others, at least for him, was to lock Johnston in by the north door and prevent another flank attempt—to give Johnston no alternative but the river. And perhaps to delay Johnston's escape until Dodge and Palmer were in place near Calhoun? Was that behind the instructions too?

Did he know of Hooker's change in plans? Was Sherman still expecting the two-pronged effort? Even if just to keep Stewart too busy to help Stevenson?

But, in the light of day, perhaps advancing between the river and the ridge looked less tempting, being a fight forward through forest toward what had not yet been seen. No one could have scouted to learn just where Hood was dug in on the other side of that ridge from the road.

Maybe, then, Sherman just wanted a demonstration—a reconnaissance in force—on that side by the railroad, to protect getting his line to the river? And to plan then the next day?

Butterfield Arrives

New York Herald: *Hooker has been employed in massing his troops under cover of the hill I have mentioned as in our possession. The divisions of Williams and Geary are ready; but Butterfield has not yet arrived. Everybody is impatient and wondering at the delay. But presently the suspense is ended as the looked-for division emerges from the woods, and moves steadily down the road.*

Captain William J. Alexander, Co D, 111th Pennsylvania, Ireland's 3rd Brigade, Geary's 2nd Division: *The corps was massed for a forward move, the 3d division in front, the 1st division on their left and our division massed by brigades in rear of the 3d.*

New York Herald: *It is now noon, and no more time is to be lost; so Butterfield being already in line, is directed to continue his march until within range, and then deploy his division in columns, by brigades, and make a charge at the enemy's position, Geary's and William's divisions to support if needed.*

On receiving his instructions, General Butterfield, who was riding at the head of his column with his staff, dashed ahead to survey the ground upon which he was to fight. Having now a clear understanding of the work he had to perform, General Butterfield was not slow in entering upon its performance.

Butterfield to Division: *Order of attack: The division will move to attack the enemy's line. The column of attack will be formed by General Ward's brigade, Colonel Coburn supporting on his right, Colonel Wood on his left. General Ward will form his column by regiment front and push a bold and vigorous attack with bayonets, a strong line of skirmishers in front. Colonel Coburn will form on his right and rear in echelon with two pieces. Colonel Wood will form on General Ward's left and rear in echelon and support, and will guard his left flank and support his assault. General Ward's column will keep well to the right of the Dalton road.*

They were to go up against the hill in column of regiments, each in two files, with about 35 paces between each regiment. The one in front, the one in the most danger—but with chance for glory—should they survive—was the 70th Indiana, led by Colonel Benjamin Harrison. He was grandson of President William Henry Harrison, famous for the Battle of Tippecanoe, but had no battle experience himself. None of Ward's regiments had ever been in battle. They rather resented it and thought Ward was to blame. But here, what they were to do was not making them enthusiastic. Would their training for mock battles during the winter under Butterfield and Hooker pay off?

On their left was to be James Wood's 1st Brigade, who had much experience fighting in the Army of the Potomac. On the right, John Coburn's 2nd Brigade, which had been marching around Kentucky and Tennessee like Ward's. But they also had a couple of skirmishes with Forrest, resulting in capture and time in Libby Prison. They were back and ready to prove themselves but did not have time for the drills and mock battles, having arrived just in time for the campaign after some long marches.

To make the assault, Hooker selected a ridge across the road which would hide and protect Butterfield's men until they started. Howard's troops were dug in along the crest. Butterfield would have to walk right over them and down the other side, across the road, and up the other hill, 800 yards open to fire from a nervously waiting enemy.

Other divisions were expected to seize the opportunity when they saw any wavering in the Rebel line.

Mouat, Co G, 29th Penn, Ireland's 3rd Brigade: *Moved about 3 miles ... here Genl Geary made a speech to us about the Glory of Pennsylvania and that the eyes of the whole Army was on us and the White Star Division, that we were to lead a charge on the Rebs works and we would be followed by supports.*

So, who was to lead the charge? Butterfield. Why was Geary telling his men they were?

But they had to wait for the wagons with their ammunition.

Hooker's intent was obvious to the waiting Confederates. There was no deception in those hours of preparation.

Abrams, Atlanta Intelligencer, with Stewart's Division, CSA: *About twelve o'clock the Yankee skirmishers opened a heavy fire on our pickets, compelling them to fall back behind the entrenchments, and at the same time heavy columns were seen forming on the right of Hindman's, Stevenson's and Stuart's divisions. There were four lines of battle in depth, and appeared to number about eight thousand men, and from the number massed in front of Stevenson's line it became apparent that his division would have to stand the brunt of the engagement. One hour passed off slowly to the gallant men who were gazing over the works in anxious expectation for the advance of the enemy.*

Last-Minute Changes

A Leg to Chew On

Howard's artillery batteries had been shelling Hood all morning and Johnston ordered Hood to move Corput's battery from behind the line, where it was protected, to a depression, a natural fort, 80 yards in front of the line. There it would be exposed and unprotected. Hood delayed, but Johnston finally gave peremptory orders. Brown's Brigade, sent four regiments, including that ever-dependable 3rd Tennessee, to the fort and they got busy piling dirt and brush in front.

Private Wes Connor, Corput's Battery: *We understood, that as soon as our guns were ready, the Confederates would charge the position occupied by the Federals on the ridge across the Dalton road, about 800 or 1000 yards on our front.*

But as the battery was being readied, a Confederate courier, Anderson, was with Hood: *It was there that Gen. Hood gave the order for the commander of a battery to stay at his guns until he and all the men were killed; not to leave the guns under any circumstances.*

Did Johnston want Corput to be a diversion? A leg for Hooker to chew on? To save the line and keep Sherman distracted?

Waiting

There is an apocryphal story of an experienced officer, on being asked why bayonet charges are not often ordered in battle, answering: *Why, if the other fellows don't run away, we do.*

The honor of leading the assault to break the key defensive point was given to a brigade with no battle experience, whose commander, Ward, was reputed to be drunk and inept. But he itched for battle. Now they waited.

Sargeant Major Fleharty, 102nd Ill, Ward's 1st Brigade: *There was evidently some warm work to be done. At first the real design of the movement was known only to a few, but when the column was formed, the men were ordered to fix bayonets, and as the ominous click ran along the line the nature of the task before us became apparent. Thought was busy then, and all faces seemed a shade paler.*

Private Henry Noble, 19th Mich, Coburn's 2nd Brigade: *Of course we privates knew nothing of the strength of their numbers and position at that time but we had a chance to test both as night set in. I cannot describe to you how I felt when I saw the battle flag and knew that we were about to go into battle but at any rate it was no very pleasant sensation that I experienced at that time.*

Lt. Colonel Merrill, 70th Ind, Ward's 1st Brigade: *At last there was a halt, and a command to unsling knapsacks and fix bayonet ... General Hooker, attended by other officers, rode forward and stated that some guns belonging to the enemy on the opposite hill were to be taken.*

For a few moments there was a stillness in which we could hear a leaf fall. No wonder, for there were men in that line who were to live but a few moments longer. Alas, not all were ready for the sacrifice! One man said 'Captain, let me fill the canteens at that spring and bring them to the boys.' Canteens nor man were ever seen again. Many a dying soldier cried in vain for water because of this cowardly perfidy. One of those, however, who looked death in the face said, 'I can feel the little hands of my babies around my neck, and hear my wife whispering goodbye.' Another, as he threw away a pack of cards: 'I don't want to be killed with these in my pocket.' Another: 'If I fall and you survive take what you find in my knapsack to mother.'

The thoughts of the older man who has left a family have a wider range than the younger. The breastworks, the rocks, the trees, the armed men sink out of sight, and the husband and father is in his Indiana home where the little children cling to him, and wife breathes what seems to be an eternal goodbye.

Sargeant Major J. L. Ketcham, 70th Indiana, Ward's 1st Brigade: *We formed in line of battle on a hill in a beautiful grove of large trees. Word was whispered down the line, 'Fix bayonets.' The order was obeyed quietly. The importance of the command seemed to be appreciated. Some of the boys told their comrades what word to send home if anything happened. It was high noon. I recollect looking at my watch and saying that my folks at home were just returning from church where they had doubtless remembered me in their prayers. I had no sense of danger in that battle. My ambition was to be the first on the enemy's breastworks. At the next battle I was not quite so ambitious.*

Captain Halstead, Co F, 79th Ohio Ward 1st Brigade: *The attacking brigade was massed in column by battalions at the foot of the hill, and advanced slowly and noiselessly, with fixed bayonets, up the hill into the thicket about 150 paces, and laid down, awaiting the order to charge. The day was excessively hot. The brigade was completely hidden, perhaps for an hour. What did they have to think about? It is not known that any one slept. Strange: so many packed together, and yet so quiet.*

Williams Deploys

Williams' 1st Division started moving to the left toward the railroad, along that little creek that ran through the plain in front of those hills. He was to deploy facing the trees from which Hood's divisions had attacked Howard last night. He started positioning artillery in the trees behind him. Robinson's brigade was on the left and Knipe's on the right, with Ruger between them. This line faced Hood's line as it bent back from the fort to the railroad.

Another Last-Minute Change

During the forenoon, Williams' division had sent Cogswell's 2nd Massachusetts on a dangerous mission to feel out the Rebel position on the hill just north of the bend in the line. That's the same hill Whitaker faced last night. They went silently and carefully till some were wounded by fire coming from the woods. So now Woods was told that his brigade, instead of supporting Ward's left, was to go first, and clear the hill on the left before Ward and Coburn could start.

Wood faced a wooded hill he had never seen and did not know what to expect. He started his regiments in column and soon found the Rebels.

Private Ryder, Co I, 33rd Mass, Wood's 3rd Brigade, Butterfield's 1st Division: *Finally, when the whole of our corps was ready, the order came, "Rise up, 33d! Guide on the colors. Forward, march!"*

We climbed the hill in our front quite quickly, the "Johnnies" retreating before we reached the top, but not so far but they could return our fire. The next man to me was struck by one of their bullets in the forehead and fell at my feet. The one the other side of me had his coat torn across from one side to the other. We lay down for a few moments until our left had come up. Then the order came, "Rise up, 33d!" For a few seconds no one moved—we just dreaded to rise—but at the second order we all sprang to our feet and jumping over the logs we rushed down the hill and up the other. Just as we reached the top where we had scarcely any protection we received the full fire from the main line of rifle pits opposite. I judged the distance to be less than 150 yards. They were expecting us and gave us a warm reception.

The hill had three tops. More Rebels were on Wood's left. He sent word to Williams. Knipe's brigade was already moving up the north side of the hill and they helped disperse those attacking Wood.

Marvin, Co F 5th Conn, Knipe's 1st Brigade, Williams' 1st Division: *About 1 P. M. The whole brigade was hastily formed and moved forward to engage the enemy. It soon became evident that a position along a crest of a hill in front must be captured, or else the line would be greatly exposed and fight under great disadvantage. The order was given to move up to this position on the double-quick, and it was given and acted upon just in time, for when the regiment arrived in position on the crest the rebel line was discovered pushing up for the same position on the opposite slope of the ridge and near at hand. The order came quickly to fire, and the first volley checked the advance of the enemy and caused them to falter and come to a halt, which gave the regiment time to load again. Upon giving them the contents of the rifles in a second volley they turned and made for their works in retreat. When the other troops saw our brigade of Red Stars come out of the woods and take that ridge and hold it and repulse the rebels, such a storm of applause went up as never before greeted it for its conduct on the battlefield.*

That applause came from Wood's brigade.

Disaster Number One

Hooker had asked for a demonstration along the line by Howard's corps, sort of a feint, to draw fire away from Hooker when the attack started. Hazen tells what happened when he started his brigade.

Hazen, 2nd Brigade, 4th Corps: *The two days we were here afforded an uninterrupted practice of sharpshooting at close range. On the second day orders were received that at twelve M., when Hooker should attack on the left, and we saw the enemy uneasy or falling back, a general attack was to be made. At the hour indicated, Hooker did attack, and the enemy's skirmishers in our front could be seen rapidly retreating, and I commanded, 'Forward'! My entire brigade leaped the works and went forward; but as no other troops did so on either of our flanks, they drew a concentrated fire of great violence and were recalled. This cost us a hundred men in less than a minute. Sixty were lost the day before in the dash to gain the ground here occupied.*

The demonstration to draw fire from Butterfield ended before the assault could get underway!

Finally—Forward!

After clearing the left hill, Wood turned south and started to cross the saddle toward the hill Ward was to attack. That's when Ward was told to start.

Merrill: *'Cheer men for Indiana! Forward! Double quick! March!' The cheers swelled into a grand shout as the whole line rushed forward!*

Benjamin Harrison's yell led Ward's regiments over the crest, over 4th Corps men who were lying down, and into the waiting Rebels' fire.

Disaster Number Two

Captain William J. Alexander, Co D, 111th Penn, Ireland's 3rd Brigade, Geary's 2nd Division: *Soon after our division moved up to their support, but as usual General John W. Geary became excited and in a very unmilitary way we were hurried to the front, passing through the lines of the 3d division.*

Spoor. Co. B, 137th NY Ireland's 3rd Brigade, Geary's 2nd Division: *Sunday the 15th we were moved over to the center and massed for a charge on a rebel battery. Everything was in readiness, and the front lines ordered forward, General Geary directing the movement in person.*

Geary sent Ireland's 3rd Brigade passing through what lines of the 3rd Division—in a very unmilitary way?

Coburn's 2nd Brigade was to go as soon as Ward cleared the ravine. But, because the ravine was so crowded, he could not arrange his lines for assault until Ward was out of the way.

Coburn, 2nd Brigade: *At the time of receiving this order to advance, and throughout the movement up the hill, the Second Division of the Twentieth Corps was moving by the left flank in from six to eight lines from right to left through my brigade, breaking and intercepting the lines, and preventing any regimental commander from seeing his own troops, or the possibility, for the time, of managing them.*

The 111th Pennsylvania was in Ireland's 3rd Brigade.

Private James Miller, 111th PA, Ireland's 3rd Brigade, Geary's 2nd Division: *When we that is our regt got within a half mile of the reb lines we came to the men of the third division all broken up and although we were the fifth line when we started the other four ran to the rear passing over and through our line but the stern order to go forward was given by Hooker in person for he was rite behind our regt and complimented us very highly for our steadiness under such circumstances.*

Here is what happened:

Engle, Co B 137th NY, Ireland's 3rd Brigade, Geary's 2nd Division: *General Geary ordered our brigade to charge a fort. We started and in a few minutes Col Ireland was in front of his brigade swinging his sword and ordering us to lay down. Geary reported him to Hooker and Thomas. They approved Irelands plan. They told Geary they didn't want their men slaughtered in no such way.*

But not all were coming back. The front regiment, the 29th Pennsylvania, kept going, not having heard the command to lie down. They went all the way across the road before they knew the rest of the brigade was not behind them.

Mouat, Co G, 29th Penn, Ireland's 3rd Brigade, Geary's 2nd Division: *We moved through the woods up a hill we had not gone far when the Rebs opened on us from three sides Killing and wounding about 70 of our Regiment in a very few minutes. … I saw a Reb flag on the breast works and I started for it I had not gone far when I heard some one shout 'Dave for Gods sake stop.' I looked back and saw Sergeant Culbertson of Company A who said Orders are to fall back as no supports are following us, we laid down and crawled back as fast as we could and soon joined our Companies, It appeared that the Johnnies had on our right and left some artillery flanked and connected by a trench in the shape of a horse shoe it was a very hot hole for while.*

They had to lay down and find their way back in little groups or one at a time.

The middle regiments that went through Coburn were so broken up they were sent out of the way. That left only two regiments to follow Butterfield's brigade if he broke the line.

Hooker himself sent Randall's 149th New York forward and they went straight on and eventually caught up with Ward. The 111th Pennsylvania, led by one of Geary's fellow Pennsylvanians, went further left into the brush, avoiding the cannon fire that got so many others in that field that had been cleared in front of the hill!

More tragedy.

Coburn had two regiments in each of his first two lines and one in his last. Somehow the 149th New York, sent ahead by Hooker, had gotten ahead of Coburn's 19th Michigan and then all passed over the soldiers laying down, presumably 4th Corps. Some were cheering them on. But some, who and why is not clear, stood up and started firing.

Noble, 19th Mich Coburn's 2nd Brigade: *There was several lines of battle in front of our reg't or Brigade when we got into position but when ordered to advance the front lines with the exception of the one in advance did not move. We were under the fire from the rebel batteries at that time and the Grape & Canister were flying around us at a rate in no wise pleasant or agreeable, and we were all lying flat on the ground. As the front lines did not stir our Brigade was ordered to charge past them and forward we went walking right over them and just as we passed the one next the front those in the rear came up behind us and without seeing a rebel commenced firing right through our lines. We were on the side of a hill and they were a little above us. This is all that saved us from being shot down by our own men. As it was there was more men in our Corps killed & wounded by this piece of carelessness than by any firing that the rebels done. It was a trying time. The smoke from the guns was almost blinding and the bullits whistled past our ears so close in some instances that they could be felt.*

Whose lines did not move?

The 149th had gotten ahead of the 19th, both going downhill by now.

Ormsby, Co E 149th NY, Ireland's 3rd Brigade, Geary's 2nd Division: *I suppose you have heard about the battle of last Sunday and who was killed or wounded in our outfit. ... Some of the companies had quite a number wounded. The doctor says that most of them were hit by the regiment that was behind us that fired into us.*

Randall, 149th NY, Ireland's 3rd Brigade, Geary's 2nd Division: *As the regiment reached the top of the hill and began to descend on the other side we received the fire of the enemy, and at that point a regiment of some other command (the Nineteenth Michigan, as I learn), which was within a few yards following us, as they received the enemy's fire, opened fire directly in our backs, severely wounding numbers of my men.*

The 149th New York, being in front, got some of the fire the 19th was getting—and blamed the 19th Michigan!

Geary was expected to follow and carry forward any success Butterfield had. Instead, he interfered with Coburn's brigade and his own 3rd Brigade became so disorganized and crowded that he could not follow as expected. Ward was already gone, Coburn was tangled up, and Ireland now had only two regiments left in the action.

Into the Fire!

Diabolical Engineering

Ward's route across the road was designed by his adversary. When they cleared the road and lower part of the hill, Confederate engineers laid out several lines of sharpened logs pointed against any attackers. Those obstacles swept around the saddle between the hills down to the front of the hill below the battery. With no way through, Hood's carefully planned route forced Hooker's columns of regiments to parade right in front of the enfilading fire of Hood's artillery. (Ample reason for Wood to come across from the other hill instead of on Ward's left.)

So, Howard's demonstration having ended with no effect:

Ritter, Rowan's Battery, Johnson's Battalion, Hood's Corps, CSA (Cummings Division): *The right of the enemy's column passed within three hundred yards of Rowan's battery, giving the latter the opportunity to open a terrific fire upon them. Many were killed and wounded, as they knew from the number of litters they saw leaving the field.*

Ward's leading regiments, the 70th Indiana and 102nd Illinois hardly slowed down despite losing many casualties. The last three regiments struggled.

Private William Grunert, Company D, 129th Illinois: *The regiments remained in pretty good line, despite the brush, and everything went on well until we came to the border of an open space, where a most murderous fire of the enemy unexpectedly saluted us. This unexpected fire, that had killed several of our men, caused some confusion in our ranks, some companies were completely disorganized, while here and there parts of regiments stood dispirited. The command lay down brought all down on the ground. After remaining there several seconds, during which the enemy's fire slackened, the command to arise was given and obeyed, when the enemy again opened on us and causing the loss of many valuable lives. We advanced some distance and again threw ourselves on the ground.*

Ward himself came back to get them going again. Then they drifted far enough left that the curvature of the hillside blocked some of the fire from the right. By then, Randall's 149th New York had caught up with them and they were joined by some scramblers from Coburn's brigade.

What became of Coburn's lines? Some regiments could not get through the confused mass crowding into them from the right and were driven further left, out of the action until much later. His 22nd Wisconsin, 20th Connecticut, and 33rd Indiana were driven so far left by Ireland and by the Confederate fire that they were headed for the ravine between the two hills.

So much crowding, so little progress. But Ward kept on, now behind his brigade, moving them on. As the first two got to the fort, Ward's last three regiments, plus some companies from Coburn and the 149th New York, closed on the others. But now all were so far left that the companies on the right got there before the others could swing around and get headed toward the fort again.

Other companies found their own problems. The upper part of the hill had trees and in front of those were piles of brush with telegraph wire strung through them. A gateway through those was well hidden, so they could not see where the enemy was except for the fire coming at them. Expecting to hit the enemy line first, the right companies found the fort and some of the left companies missed it.

Into the Fort!

As soon as they crossed the road and cleared the obstacles, the column had drifted left, away from the cannon fire and perhaps to some cover under the curve of the hillside. But they still had to keep their front facing the fort. Their lines were also getting bunched up. As they got close they found themselves too far left and had to swing their left companies around. So:

Colonel Case, 129th Illinois: *When the actual charge into and through the fort was made the charging party consisted of parts of the right companies of each regiment in the brigade, the rear regiments having in the mean time closed upon the head of the column.*

CJH, Brown's Brigade, Stevenson's Division, Hood's Corp, CSA: *A position being selected fifty yards in advance of the left wing of our command for Corput's battery of twelve pound Napoleons, numbering four guns; by the engineers redoubts were being hastily thrown up, when about twelve o'clock the enemy's skirmishers opened a heavy fire upon our pickets, driving them on their line of battle, following so closely that the 32d Tennessee, working upon the redoubt, found themselves suddenly opposed to a line of Yankees within a few rods of them, and were compelled to fight their way back to the intrenchments, hand to hand with picks, spades and rocks, the enemy planting their colors upon the battery, but unable to remove it, the 32d and 26th Tennessee regiments, commanded by the gallant Colonels Cook and Saffree, resisting every effort made. The country in our front was thickly wooded and covered with dense undergrowth, concealing their advance until very near; under this cover they had massed their troops in immense numbers and advanced cautiously in their lines of battle until sufficiently near, when they burst upon us with a loud hurrah.*

Wesley Connor, private, Cherokee Artillery, CSA: *Between one and two o'clock the Federals brought out a line on said ridge as if preparing for an advance, and we pitched into them with our guns, and were giving them the best we had, when the first thing we knew the pickets came running past our guns with the announcement that the Yankees were right on us—some of them had passed our first gun before I left my gun—(I was gunner of #2, the guns being numbered from right to left) in fact two or three of them were parting the brush in front of my gun, and I shall never forget how they looked as they came through. Each of them seemed to be about ten feet tall and big in proportion. I left my gun double shotted with canister, as two friction primers in succession had failed to do their work. Our supporting infantry, Gen. John C. Brown's Brigade of Tennesseans, were as much surprised as we were, and barely had time to get into the trenches in time to stop your advance This will explain why our battery overshot you.*

Lt. Col. Merrill, 70th Ind, Ward's 1st Brigade: *The cannon in the lunette thundered a reply, but there was no stopping till all the gunners but five were either killed or taken prisoners. For a little while there was a wild scene in the lunette, artillery men defending their guns, Union officers firing their pistols, and the men their rifles; now using their bayonets, now clubbing their muskets, now leaping on the cannon and waving their hats. The infantry in the works beyond the fort, seized with a panic, left their coats and spades in the trench where they had been working, and disappeared for the time through the woods in the rear.*

Col. Harrison 70th Ind, Ward's 1st Brigade: *The men moved on with perfect steadiness and without any sign of faltering up the hillside and to the very muzzles of the enemy's artillery, which continued to belch their deadly charges of grape and canister, until the gunners were struck down at their guns. Having gained the outer face of the embrasures, in which the enemy had four 12-pounder Napoleon guns, my line halted for a moment to take breath. Seeing that the infantry supports had deserted the artillery, I cheered the men forward, and with a wild yell they entered the embrasures, striking down and bayoneting the rebel gunners, many of whom defiantly stood by their guns till struck down. Within this outer fortification, in which the artillery was placed, there was a strong line of breastworks, which was concealed from our view by a thick pine undergrowth, save at one point, which had been used as a gateway. This line was held by a rebel division of veteran troops, said to be of Hood's command. When we first entered the embrasures of the outer works the enemy fled in considerable confusion from the inner one, and had there been a supporting line brought up in good order at this juncture the second line might have easily been carried and held. My line having borne the brunt of the assault, it was not to be expected that it could be reformed for a second assault in time.*

One person on the left was so far ahead he missed the fort—he went right past it and found Brown's part of the main line!

Sergeant Major J. L. Ketcham, 70th Indiana, Ward's Brigade: *After I entered the thicket I noticed nothing until I found myself on the enemy's breastworks. Evidently these breastworks protected rebel infantry supporting their artillery. But where were the infantry? I stood some moments wondering what had become of them. I could see every evidence of their having been there; their fires were burning for cooking; their haversacks and knapsacks were there. I thought I could hear them stampeding down the hill. The breastworks were in a semicircle and obstructed my view. Why did not our boys come? I shouted 'Come on!' Then I realized that I was alone and that my comrades had been drawn by the sound of the cannon to the right. I hastened in the same direction to shout my discovery. The thicket was dense. I could only see a few feet ahead of me.*

So, they almost had success better than anyone expected, but Ketcham alone knew. No one behind them knew Butterfield's brigades had broken the line! Hooker and Howard saw only smoke!

About ten minutes, by one measure, maybe twenty. That's how long it took to clear the Rebels out of the fort—and their trench behind it too. It was a victory for Hooker—if he could keep it. Where were the others, those who were to follow them and carry the line Harrison had broken?

Disaster Number Three

Wood's 3rd Brigade got caught in the mess. On his right, Winkler's 26th Wisconsin extended down into the ravine. Winkler had watched Ward's brigade cross the road to go up the hill next to him. Then:

Col. Winkler, 26th Wis, Wood's 3rd Brigade: *Another line of battle broke forth from the woods on the right of the road into the open field in front & then pushed obliquely to the left across the road & came directly in front of my line ... Col. Wood just passing by in rear of my regiment I called his attention to them. The line which came up behind me did not halt but passed right over my men & pushed forward into the thicket in my front where it was at once concealed from my sight.*

Harrison was leaning on a cannon, conversing, when a bullet came through his beard.

Stevenson had gathered up his panicked soldiers and they came forward, firing!

Captain Meredith: 70th Ind: *The second line of Federals, partially encountering the rebel fire, deliver a volley and the soldiers of the first line, who had led the charge, who had driven the enemy and captured the guns, are literally caught between two fires.*

Col. Dustin, 105th Ill: *While the line rested for a moment under the works a shower of musketry came upon us from the left and rear, and instantly a command was heard (since learned to have been given by a rebel officer), 'We are flanked! March in retreat!'*

Col. Dustin, 105th Ill: *Supposing the order to have been given by the proper authority, the brigade fell back, with the exception of those officers and men who had got into the fort or were sheltered by it on the outside.*

Col. Winkler, 26th Wis, Wood's 3rd Brigade: *A heavy musketry fire immediately opened in my front & a large number of troops came rushing back in disorder through my line & lay down behind it.*

That inexperienced regiment found themselves being fired on and, seeing only smoke, returned fire—into the fort.

Captain Meredith: 70th Ind: *The scene the terror of the moment is beyond description. The cry went up: Our own men are firing into us. When the panic was at its greatest, one or two officers who were in the captured redoubt shouted the command, 'Lie down!' and about one hundred and fifty men crouched behind the earthworks containing the guns, and began skirmishing with the enemy.*

The Rebels had regained their line. Many of the men who captured the fort evacuated and huddled outside with the rest of their regiments. Harrison and some men had found a ledge to protect them.

Wounded in front by enemy and in back by foe, those in the fort were suddenly trapped.

Trapped!

Ward had been slightly wounded on the way but caught up only to find about 300 hundred trapped in the fort. Inside, he tried to organize another attack on the Rebel line. But a captain of the 129th Illinois told him *For God's sake, general, don't fire; those are our men in those works!* They tried moving forward, but any time they moved firing started again. Ward was wounded again. All they could do was lay flat.

Stalemate

According to his timeline, Howard's 4th Corps adjutant was told at 2:20 pm that Hooker had secured a lodgment.

Gen. Fullerton, Adjutant, 4th Corp: *At this time General Whitaker's brigade, of Stanley's division, was in the rear of Hooker, waiting orders to advance, while Schofield's command was acting as an immediate support.*

Whitaker was never sent.

Now the battle for the north was a stalemate. Any attempt by either side failed. Rebel snipers were busy targeting those in or around the fort. The opportunity was gone. The fort had been a distraction. It was a leg to chew on, keeping Hooker's men from their original objective: to break the line. Howard and Geary could do nothing.

No help from below:

Col. Pardee, 147th PA, Candy's 1st Brigade, Geary's 2nd Divsion: *The battalions being closed in mass they were set in motion by the commanding officer of the brigade, under the personal superintendence of the division commander, and ordered to take the fort at all hazards. I can only say that I did not see the fort and do not think my command was within 200 yards of it when I halted, being unable to pass over the numerous lines of troops in my front, of which I had no knowledge at the time of starting, without breaking my line and thus rendering it useless in the charge. Under orders ... I withdrew my regiment under cover of the ridge over which we had just passed.*

Geary's white stars were blocked by the milling mass, but they still had their weapons and were surely getting hits from the firing above. Firing back, uphill, at the smoke, was not helpful.

Lieutenant W. R. McCracken, 70th Ind: *After the Seventieth Indiana and the brigade of which it was a part had taken the battery and were holding it under a terrible fire from the enemy, a musketry fire was poured into them from the rear. Colonel Harrison ordered me to see what the firing meant. I found that it came from a body of our own men belonging to the Second Division, who were behind some timber. I told them to stop firing or the First Brigade would have to retire from the works they had taken and were holding. The firing was stopped, but by the time I was back to my command it began again. Colonel Harrison then directed me to go back and hunt up General Butterfield, who commanded the Third Division, and tell him of the firing from the rear, and that the Brigade would have to fall back if it was not stopped. I could not find Butterfield, but found General Williams, commanding the*

First Division, and inquired for General Butterfield and told him what I wanted. General Williams said he did not know where General Butterfield was, but told me where to find General Hooker, who, on being informed, spurred his horse and rode rapidly to the place where the white star troops lay, and the firing ceased.

Geary sent some of his regiments filing up the ravine to help hold the fort. Later he sent some more in a regimental front. That aroused more fire since the Confederates thought they were another wave of attackers. Amidst that distraction, many of Ward's men in the fort escaped in little groups as best they could.

Coburn and many of his 2nd Brigade remained, as did some of Ward's.

Col. Coburn, 2nd Brigade: *Soon after my arrival at the immediate vicinity of the rebel works General Ward was wounded and left the field. I took command of the forces there and made three efforts to charge and take the enemy's works, but such was the disorganized condition of the men of both brigades and the terrific force of their fire that each charge failed and nothing more could be done than hold the place up to the line of their breast-works. In one of these charges late in the day the One hundred and eleventh Pennsylvania, Colonel Cobham, gallantly participated.*

Fighting back and forth continued in front of the fort and around the nose of the hill on the left for some time, with neither side making progress. The 5th Connecticut was in an open space.

Captain Marvin, Co F 5th Conn, Knipe's 1st Brigade, Williams' 1st Division: *Amidst the storm of shot and shell, the regiment commenced singing the Battle Cry of Freedom, which was taken up by the troops on the right and left. The color guard (brave men) advanced well to the front, waving Old Glory in the faces of the Confederates. The effect was magical, and one must have been there and witnessed the scene in order to appreciate the inspiration and enthusiasm aroused from so simple and common an incident. The enemy continued to charge time after time, but found that the sentiment of that Battle Cry, backed up by the rifles of the brave men of the First Brigade, were too much for them, and so they retired from such a losing contest and the battle ended. It was one of the many square fights in the open field, without breastworks or defenses of any kind, which the regiment was called upon to fight during its service, and was an achievement of which the regiment was ever afterwards deservedly proud. But the battle was not won without severe loss. Company K was at the extreme left of the regiment, and during a part of the engagement at the extreme left of the whole line of battle, and received a terrible fire both from front and left flank. There were but about thirty men in that company that day, and fifteen of them fell killed or wounded in less than ten minutes of that terrible ordeal; yet the other fifteen stood as staunch and firm at their posts as when they first took their position on that fatal ridge. With such metal alone can victories be hewn.*

The Gambit

Hood had held. Hooker seemed to be out of moves. Paramount for Johnston: do not get trapped!

For all Johnston knew, Walker's Division was keeping Sweeny at bay at Lay's Ferry. Butterfield was bloodied in a vain failure to break Hood. Geary was busy moving men up to replace them outside the fort. Hovey's division of Schofield's 23rd Corps, two regiments of raw Indiana recruits, was expected to work their way beyond the railroad to the river but apparently were not there yet.

Stewart's Division had been unmolested through all this, and Stevenson still had two brigades in reserve.

Could Hood now work around Howard? Then what? Could he follow up without splitting his line? Might he at least keep Hooker and Howard occupied? Keep Sherman from sending more men against Polk? Or even to Grant? Reduce the odds at the river-crossing by drawing men north?

What was on Johnston's mind?

They're Coming!

Left of the fort, at the angle of the line, Geary's 149th New York noticed something:

Captain Collins, 149th NY Ireland's 3rd Brigade, Geary's 2nd Division: *About four o'clock, ... the 149th men, with their companions lying on the hillside, could hear the Confederates forming in line and their well-known yell in charging, but could not see the movement owing to intervening woods. As the enemy advanced no opposition seemed to be interposed until he was well in rear of the line held by the men below the little fort.*

Wood's brigade was still holding in the saddle between the hills, facing Stevenson. They had been under fire all this time.

Captain Osborn, Co A 55th Ohio, Wood's 3rd Brigade: *At last the writer heard Captain H. E. Tremain, a volunteer aide on General Butterfield's staff, calling out to 'Colonel Wood, Sir, you must not expose yourself in this way.' But, said Colonel Wood, in his high-pitched voice, 'I want to see what they are doing; they are getting out of their works.' It proved to be true. The Fifty-fourth Virginia Regiment of infantry formed under that terrific fire and charged our line. It was, of course, captured to a man and was hurried to the rear, where the captives saw to their disgust the Second Division of the Twentieth Corps massed in support of the fighting line and the Twenty-third Corps moving up on the left flank.*

Stewart and Stevenson were to have wheeled out together at 4 o'clock. Stewart's trench was in the trees, well back of Williams, while Stevenson was right in front of Knipe and Wood. And Stewart had to arrange his brigades, holding his left steady till his right could swing around, before advancing.

But Stevenson got peremptory orders. One brigade was replenishing ammunition. Only the 54th Virginia (and maybe another regiment) leaped the trenches and rushed bravely upon the enemy. They got clobbered and, finding no connection with General Stewart's left, fell back.

When Stewart started—with his left exposed, Williams was waiting.

Colgrove's Ambush

Around the hill, facing the woods on the east side, Williams had placed artillery behind him and was digging in, getting ready for the action to come to him. Robinson's brigade was on the left, close to the railroad, with only two regiments in the front. Ruger's brigade was spread out right of Robinson, connecting with Knipe.

Colonel Colgrove, of the 27th Indiana on Ruger's right, connecting with Knipe's brigade, rode forward to see why his skirmishers were firing. They pointed to enemy skirmishers coming out of the trees. Stewart was forming in line to charge. Colgrove quietly moved his regiment halfway forward and hid them below a slight rise. The 2nd Massachusetts followed suit.

Corporal Edmund Brown, Co C 27th Indiana Ruger's 2nd Brigade, Williams' 1st Division: *At the command the whole line was to rise up, fire a careful, deliberate volley into the ranks of the advancing enemy, then charge them with the bayonet. ... At length, when the rebel force was only thirty-five yards away, the Colonel, speaking in slow, distinct tones, said, 'Now, boys. Ready, aim, fire!' Then he fairly shrieked the one word 'Charge!' and all the other officers repeated the word, with deeply surcharged feelings, 'Charge!' Poor men of the misguided South! It was all over in one terrible minute of time.*

Round one to Ruger. Colgrove's men scrambled back and waited. Then another round to Ruger. When they came a third time, Ruger's left regiments advanced and his right regiments wheeled and caught them in a crossfire.

Corporal Edmund Brown, Co C 27th Indiana Ruger's 2nd Brigade, Williams' 1st Division: *Our advance at this time was to within fifty yards of the enemy's works. Many of our brigade have always believed firmly that their line might have been driven, if not routed, at this time.*

That possibility, unknown to Brown, was more real than he could have realized.

Ridley's Ride

Expecting to die any second, Stewart's aide, Captain Ridley, was dodging cannon fire, racing his horse back and forth between Stewart's brigades, trying to tell them to call it off! About noon, when Butterfield was getting ready to start, Dodge had gotten two brigades across the Oostanaula and was getting a second pontoon bridge across. Johnston thought Walker's Division was working to force them back. But now, too late, he knew instead that more would come.

Stewart's men were disorganized, trying to return to their trenches.

Captain Ridley, Stewart's Division, Hood's Corps, CSA: *There was one place, though, where Sherman, had he been the able general many supposed, would have taken some of Johnston's glory from him. The only time he ever got Johnston apparently in a nine hole was at Resaca on May 15, 1864.*

Missed Opportunity

There must be many military maxims about opportunity coming to those who are prepared, or, more to the point, about being ready for the unexpected. And here it came—thought of last night but then discarded—forfeited!

General Williams, 1st Division, 20th Corps: *I made no efforts to pursue, as my orders were to cover and protect the left, and I was ignorant of the condition of affairs with the assaulting columns on the right ...*

... besides, the enemy's intrenchments, to which at each repulse he fell back, were but a few hundred yards in my front. It was evident, too, that the assaulting force (at least two divisions of Hood's corps) greatly outnumbered ours.

And thus he was not aware that Butterfield's attack had for a moment rolled back Stevenson's line. What would have been the result had Hood been attacked simultaneously on both sides of the ridge at this point?

According to Brown, those attacks by Stewart were kept up too long for late news of Sweeny's crossing to have been the delay.

Corporal Edmund Brown, Co C 27th Indiana Ruger's 2nd Brigade, Williams' 1st Division: *The engagement along our front continued for at least an hour and a half. During all of this time the enemy was acting upon the offensive. Though not resolute or determined to a marked degree, he still manifested some spirit and persistence. If the battle was brought on under a misapprehension, that it should be continued as a losing fight for so long, or that it should require so much time for those in control to come to an understanding among themselves, seems mysterious. Whatever may be the facts, however, on this point, it was certainly fortunate for them that other troops were not put in. To have doubled the force against Williams' division, or to have doubled the enthusiasm back of the assault, would only have doubled the loss sustained, and the disappointment of defeat. The assault as it was, was so very ineffectual, so very far from the least sign of success, that it is impossible to conjecture what might have rendered it otherwise. Not over half of Williams' division took any part in the battle, and those that did take part were only getting fairly at it when the battle was over.*

Could it be that those little assaults were just to keep Williams from assaulting while Stewart covered his pullback? Or was he tempting Williams to charge further—to Stewart's back line?

Hood himself answers: *I shall always believe the attack of Stevenson's and Stewart's Divisions, therein described ... saved us from utter destruction by creating the impression upon the Federals that the contest was to be renewed the next morning.*

Indeed, Hooker, by his assault, convinced Johnston that he had little time to waste getting out of Resaca. He knew time was up when Dodge got established near Calhoun.

And, ironically, Johnston had kept Hooker, Howard, and Schofield occupied two miles away—all day.

Night came. Darkness covered the battle line.

Clack's Ruse

You cannot see a quietly waiting adversary as you work up to the crest of a hill. But as soon as the top of your head appears he will have it in his sights. All alone, hidden behind burning logs that lit up the fort and anyone peering over the edge, Hood left Lt. Colonel Clack's indispensable 3rd Tennessee. And while Thomas was re-arranging his artillery for the next day and things were deceptively quiet on the south, Clack's thinned ranks made enough distraction to convince Hooker that Hood's divisions were still there and ready to attack.

The Bait

Men had died trying to get those guns. They were not going to give them up. They had to justify the dying. Clack said, in effect, if you want them come and get them. Thus the 3rd, by themselves, held three corps close by the lure of something Johnston was willing to sacrifice in order to get out of Resaca.

Storrs, 20th Conn, Coburn's 2nd Brigade: *During the evening, Lieut. Colonel Buckingham of the 20th Connecticut was detailed to take command of a detachment of troops. ... The detachment moving out about 9 p.m. after groping around in the dark, found the position and formed around the side of the hill below the battery. Lieut. Colonel Buckingham, accompanied by Captain Doolittle of the 20th, proceeded to reconnoitre and examine the location in order to determine upon a course of action.*

Lt. Col. Buckingham, 20th Conn, Coburn's 2nd Brigade: *Creeping on our hands and knees over the dead bodies thickly strewn about, we reached the lunette and found a Second division man lying flat on his face in front of the earthworks, behind which the guns were. We placed our hands on the muzzles of the guns that protruded from the embrasures, and after crawling about the front, of the entrenched battery to get a correct knowledge of the situation, one of the officers accompanying me raised his hat on the point of his sword above the earthworks and received a shower of bullets as a reply, two or three passing through his hat.*

Storrs, 20th Conn, Coburn's 2nd Brigade: *The result of which was that two plans were presented for the accomplishment of the object. One was that of Colonel Cobham, of the 2d Division, who advocated a charge against the main works of the enemy, under cover of which the guns should be run over toward the Rebel lines and round the end of the bluff on which they were situated and into the Union lines. The other, that of Lieut. Colonel Buckingham, was to dig them out, and this latter course was adopted. Commencing some two or three rods down the hill, a trench was dug toward the muzzle of each piece, wide enough to admit the passage of the gun carriages. About 2 o'clock ropes were attached to the pieces and they were dragged silently through the trenches down the hill and into the Union lines. The battery proved to have been composed of four nice, new, brass twelve pounders, only just out of the arsenal at Augusta. The guns were found loaded with a double charge of grape shot. The mission was accomplished without the loss of a man. The Rebels seemed to have been aware that some movement was in progress for the capture of the guns and several times during the night started in with quite a brisk fire, in the direction of the works.*

Colonel Clack's clear, ringing voice aided the deception: *Hold your fire, men, do not waste your ammunition, let them come closer.*

Sergeant Major Fleharty, 102nd Ill, Ward's 1st Brigade: *Towards evening it was feared the battery would be retaken. One by one the men began to retire, notwithstanding the expostulations of those who remained. After dark the enemy opened a sharp fire, as if menacing a charge to retake the guns. A volley was fired in return; the boys yelled out a defiant cheer, and one shouted to the Johnnies: 'Come over and take your brass field pieces!' Help had been sent for, and at length we heard music in the valley below. Sweet as the music of heaven, soothing the soul after the harrowing, discordant day of battle. Inwoven with our very beings, the ecstatic sensations of that moment, when the soft, plaintive, but cheering notes of a field band were borne to our ears, will live in memory forever. We learned afterwards, however, that the music did not herald the approach of a relieving column, but relief soon came.*

They were replacements that Geary had sent.

Private Denniston, 33rd NJ, Mindil's 2nd Brigade, Geary's 2nd Division: *It was a lovely moonlight night, and one of our bands was playing Yankee Doodle.*

Then Clack slipped away, the last across the river, leaving a hill littered with dead and wounded. By far, most were from Ward's brigade and most of those from Harrison's regiment.

Corporal Blakeslee, Co G 129th Ill, Ward's 1st Brigade: *Capt, J. H. Culver [Company A, 129th Illinois] who led the boys beyond the captured guns … held the position until only 27 men were left with him, each and every one whom should have a medal. He held the fort and captured battery until relieved at 10 o'clock p.m. the only protection afforded him being the dead body of Capt. Blackburn, Co. A, 79th Ohio, whose blood saturated his clothing from chin to boots.*

Company A normally being the rightmost company of a regiment, both men would have been in the first storming parties. They had been there ever since, the living protected by the dead.

Geary clung to the hill.

Colonel Lane, 102nd NY, Ireland's 3rd Brigade Geary's 2nd Division: *We held this position without relief (or a chance of making coffee) until 2 oclock the next morning.*

When the sun rose, Johnston's army was past Calhoun. They left their seriously wounded to the care of the Federal army.

Hooker got the guns, Johnston got away, and Sherman got left behind.

AFTERMATH

Sergeant Major Fleharty, 102nd Ill, Ward's 1st Brigade: *The scene on the battle-ground the following day was sad beyond description. The day was calm indeed the stillness was oppressive. We were permitted to wander over the field and view the effects of the fierce struggle.*

General Stanley, 1st Division, 4th Corps: *Johnston took an immense risk in fighting north of the Oostanula. A single break in his line and his army was lost.*

Stone, Thomas' staff: *Some idea of the strength of Johnston's position, and the character of his works, may be drawn from a remark of General Poe, Sherman's Chief Engineer, after he had made a careful inspection on the morning of the 16th. Yesterday, he said, I was afraid they would run away. To-day, after what I have seen, I find I ought to have been afraid they wouldn't.*

Blundin, Co C, 28th Penn, Candy's 1st Brigade, Geary's 2nd Division: *Hulmsville, Pa I remember the day well, as our brigade (the First of the Second Division) was in line with the intention of charging that same four-gun fort; but the other troops got in their work first, and we had to stand and see them do their work, and grandly they did it. Talking to some of them after they had made their successful charge, I was informed that the brigade was under the command of Col. Ben Harrison, ... I witnessed the charge of the brigade, of which Col. Harrison was the commander ... and I am under the impression now as then that said fort was the key of the rebel line. It was certainly an effective charge.*

General Stanley: *There is no doubt that Joseph Johnston's army was in a perilous position here and, if Hooker's assault the next day had been supported, the rebel army would have been destroyed. They were terribly frightened and from where I stood I could see the Rebel right from which men were running away by the hundreds.*

Sergeant Major Ketcham, 70th Indiana, Ward's 1st Brigade: *That we were not fired into by the Rebels from behind their intrenchments for ten minutes after taking the guns, proves the statement of a prisoner that a whole Rebel brigade behind those works threw down their guns and ran, found we didn't follow, rallied and gave us fits. What a sad mistake in not advancing! But we did not know, thought that all there was to be done was to take the guns.*

Mrs. Porter, Sanitary Commission: *Never have I passed such a Sabbath as yesterday, and I wish I could believe there never would be such another ... The wounded were brought into hospitals, quickly and roughly prepared in the forest, as near the field as safety would permit ... What a scene was presented! Precious sons of northern mothers, beloved husbands of northern wives were already here to undergo amputation, to have wounds probed and dressed, or broken limbs and bandaged. Some were writhing under the surgeon's knife, but bore their suffering bravely and uncomplainingly. ... Never was the presence of women more joyfully welcomed. It was touching to see those precious boys looking up into our faces with such hope and gladness. It brought to their minds mother and home, as each testified while his wounds were being dressed; This seems a little like having mother about, was the reiterated expression of the wounded, as one after another was washed and had his wounds dressed. Mrs. Bickerdyke and myself assisted in the operation. Poor boys! how my heart ached that I could do so little. ... We found what we brought in the ambulance was giving untold comfort to our poor exhausted wounded men, whose rough hospital couches were made by pine boughs with the stems cut out. spread upon the ground, over which their blankets were thrown. This forms the bed, and the poor fellows' blouses, saturated with their own blood. is their only pillow, their knapsacks being left behind when they went into battle ... Several wounded men have died during the night.*

Lt. Col. Merrill, 70th Ind, Ward's 1st Brigade: *It was a strange grave by which the surviving members stood. It was six feet long and sixty wide. Into this, side by side, with blankets for winding sheets, were lowered the forms of those who had just died for their country. Evergreen branches were tenderly dropped on the sleeping patriots, to break the fall of the clods, and as a token that their sacrifice would ever be green in the memory of their comrades. With heads uncovered the mourners gathered about the grave. The Captains of the companies cast in the first earth, and the Chaplain prayed that the sad tidings might not crush the hearts of the mothers, the widows and the orphans. The sinking sun closed the mournful day, and the dead were left to sleep in their glory, while to the living remained the stern duty of pursuing through the night the retreating battalions of the enemy.*

Members of regimental bands have more to do than have fun playing music and waking the soldiers in the morning. During battle they risk their lives bearing stretchers of the wounded off the field. Then they march on, playing the survivors to their next battle.

Benton, Band, 150th NY, Ruger's 2nd Brigade, Williams' 1st Division: *The turkey buzzards, with their sooty, dishevelled plumage and filthy beaks, were circling lower and lower over the field, but the Pioneer Corps were busy now burying the dead, both of the Blue and the Gray, while the wounded were being got away to the North. So these North American vultures would feast this time only on dead horses. Youth and Hope go hand in hand and will not be depressed, and as we pushed on after the enemy we laughed and joked as before.*

FIGHTING TO ATLANTA

Nearing Atlanta after many hard-fought battles, Harrison, Coburn, and Wood, on their own initiatives, took their brigades up a ridge in the Battle of Peach Tree Creek to plug a gap that Ward, now commanding the division, had allowed by negligence and through which Hood was attempting another Chickamauga. Ireland also took his brigade forward and at great loss pushed back an attempt to flank Geary.

Hooker resigned after General McPherson was killed near Atlanta and Sherman gave command of the Army of the Tennessee to Howard, Hooker's junior, who Hooker blamed for his defeat at Chancellorsville.

Mrs. Bickerdyke and Mrs. Porter nursed the wounded for five months, all the way from Resaca to Atlanta. The campaign cost 32,000 Union casualties and 35,000 Confederate.

John Coburn had the honor of accepting surrender from the mayor of Atlanta in September. Then Lincoln won the election in all states but one. The Confederacy was doomed.

TO THE END

After the defeat at Atlanta, Hood still had 40,000 men—and invaded the north! On October 13, he threatened to annihilate the entire garrison at Resaca if they did not surrender. Defied, he moved on. Thomas waited at Nashville and crushed Hood's army in two days of battle in icy weather.

Harrison was with Thomas, commanding a brigade of detached regiments, and did not get back to his original brigade until the war was over. Case commanded in Harrison's absence.

Leaving Thomas to fight Hood, Sherman went on to Savannah and then North Carolina, with Williams commanding 20th Corps. Slocum commanded the new Army of Georgia, Sherman's left wing, and Howard commanding Army of the Tennessee, the right wing.

In April, Lee surrendered to Grant and then Johnston to Sherman.

Harrison was elected U. S. President, helped by his achievement at Resaca. Geary served two terms as Pennsylvania governor but did not live to seek the presidency he craved.

CAMPFIRES

This book is taken from the writings in *They All Wore a Star*, which are footnoted there and listed in a bibliography. Albert Castell's *Decision in the West* should be consulted for details of the battle this book does not cover.

The best way to read *They All Wore a Star* is to imagine you are at a reunion many years after the battle. Night after night, you, along with the author as your guide, stop by their campfires and listen to them share vivid memories. *They All Wore a Star* is actual quotes from those who were in the battle, arranged according to location and chronology as best makes sense. The latter is difficult because often one writer had a limited view, it being only what he could see from his position. And their sense of time by the clock varied wildly. The author matched the stories by their location relative to others on the battlefield and then provided limited narrative to relate those stories and guide the reader. But it is quite rich reading in the sense that you are hearing from those who went through it—they are first-hand accounts, not digestions or heresay rehashes by third parties. Within their stories are many that do not make it into historical interpretations but stand on their own worth for the time spent reading them. Together, they tell much more than the histories even though they are not altogether consistent. No two witnesses ever tell the same details. But omitting them is a greater sin because they are still revealing even if they do not fit together nicely.

Thus, these original sources have been selected according to Abraham Lincoln's admonition to a jury: *There is some conflict of testimony in the case, but one quarter of such a number of witnesses, seldom agree, and even if all had been on one side some discrepancy might have been expected. We are to try and reconcile them, and to believe that they are not intentionally erroneous, as long as we can.*

With that in mind, here are some first-hand tales that you will not find together in any other one place.

Amusing dialog between Mary Ann Bickerdyke and General Sherman after she took the train to Chattanooga and barged into his office and quickly shamed him out of two train cars a day to supply the wounded.

Sergeant Morhouse's attempt to tell the range of emotions while heading for battle, unable to return fire while standing elbow to elbow with comrades getting hit by cannon and musket, then charging and killing, and finally tending the wounded, friend and foe alike.

General Williams attempting to describe battle for his daughter.

And his description of what it takes to supply an enormous army in war.

Sergeant Sam Peak's tale of finding sweet potatoes in a haystack, while scouting for guerillas in Kentucky, and capturing a notorious guerilla leader too.

Sam Peak's ride down Cumberland Mountain at night on a train with burning brakes and catching sight of what was left of previous wrecks flying by.

Robert Hale Strong and others describing finding their way down Cumberland Mountain at night with no road, lifting wagons through mud and over ledges, after General Ward got them lost and then left it for Colonel Harrison to get them out.

The dispute, waged in official records, correspondence, and forums as late as 1885, about who captured the guns, Geary or Harrison.

Corporal Blakeslee getting captured by guerillas and forced to accompany them on a train raid, then turned loose where they found him and allowed to keep the uniform he ordered from Chicago for $85. And many other incidents dealing with guerillas in Kentucky.

The terrible marches of the 129th Illinois to catch up with Bragg's army in Kentucky, losing many men, some permanently, but not getting there in time for two battles.

The effect on the soldiers after seeing the results of Perryville and Stones Creek, and then marching through the battleground of Chickamauga at the beginning of the campaign.

General Geary's sheer luck in getting his division under the noses of pickets to cross Chattanooga Creek in order to attack Lookout Mountain, for which he took full credit.

Wes Connor's effort to shoot a Union sniper after he escaped from the fort, ending with splinters of his gun stock in his jaw.

Thomas' men storming Missionary Ridge to avoid being easy targets when attempting to just draw fire from Sherman's men. Their unintended attack so surprised the Confederates that they withdrew, ending the Battle for Chattanooga.

Captain Halstead's droll tale of Private George Totten, "The Hero of Resaca", and of Totten later leading a division in the Battle of Averasbrough.

Many accounts of the fighting in the fort.

Freezing in the rain in February while marching from Nashville to Wauhatchie.

John Coburn's efforts to protect slaves who had sought shelter in camp. And his pre-war efforts on behalf of free negros in Indiana.

What toughens a soldier to survive, according to Adjutant Boyle.

Sergeant Frederick Hess of the 129th Illinois, already wounded, carrying their flag and planting it by one of the guns before finally being killed.